ISLAMIC AND ETHICAL FINANCE IN THE UNITED KINGDOM

ISLAMIC AND ETHICAL FINANCE IN THE UNITED KINGDOM

Elaine Housby

EDINBURGH
University Press

© Elaine Housby, 2013

Edinburgh University Press Ltd
22 George Square, Edinburgh EH8 9LF
www.euppublishing.com

Typeset in Minion Pro by
Servis Filmsetting Ltd, Stockport, Cheshire,
and printed and bound in Great Britain by
CPI Group (UK) Ltd, Croydon CR0 4YY

A CIP record for this book is available from the British Library

ISBN 978 0 7486 4896 2 (hardback)
ISBN 978 0 7486 4895 5 (paperback)
ISBN 978 0 7486 4897 9 (webready PDF)
ISBN 978 0 7486 7826 6 (epub)

The right of Elaine Housby to be identified as author of this
work has been asserted in accordance with the Copyright,
Designs and Patents Act 1988.

Published with the support of the Edinburgh University
Scholarly Publishing Initiatives Fund.

CONTENTS

A NOTE ON THE TERM 'UNITED KINGDOM'

The United Kingdom consists of England, Wales, Scotland and Northern Ireland. Great Britain consists of England, Wales and Scotland. It is not strictly speaking correct to use the terms Britain and the UK interchangeably, but it is common practice to do so and this book follows this common practice. There are important differences in the law and government of the component parts of the UK and thus in the availability of financial services. Providers will sometimes speak of their products being available 'in the UK' when they are in fact only available in England and Wales.

Now that a referendum on the possible independence of Scotland has been announced, the survival of the United Kingdom in its present form is not certain. Even if full independence is rejected, there is no doubt that Scotland will become more important as a centre of Islamic finance in its own right. It has been estimated that, as a proportion of GDP, financial services form a larger part of the economy of Scotland than of the UK as a whole. The present Scottish parliament sees significant opportunities in developing expertise in Islamic finance and closer links with the Muslim majority world. Capacity building in both Islamic and ethical finance is being actively pursued by a number of agencies and companies in Scotland, including the Islamic Finance Council based in Glasgow. The differences between Scottish and English law, particularly in the area of property rights, will therefore become increasingly salient to the Islamic financial sector in the UK.[1]

These differences are mostly not relevant to the present book, but readers overseas should at least be aware of their existence.

Note

1. Any readers wishing to learn more about these differences will find a convenient summary in: Houston, Rab (2008), *Scotland: A Very Short Introduction*, Oxford: Oxford University Press.

CHAPTER 1
INTRODUCTION

Discussion of the term 'ethical'

Islamic finance is routinely described as ethical. This reflects the fact that self-described 'ethical' finance is a large and growing sector of the market. It has a very positive image with which Islamic financial services seek to associate themselves. The claim that 'Islamic' and 'ethical' are synonymous is rarely seriously examined, and nor is the claim that there exists a consistent and generally understood definition of 'ethical' practice. The case studies in this book have been chosen because they shed light on the difficulties of arriving at a consensus definition of what 'ethical' means and of positioning the Islamic sector as a sub-set of the ethical sector. At its worst the term 'ethical' has become little more than a marketing label. This detailed consideration of providers which all position themselves as 'ethical' is intended to get beyond this to see what the term means in the diverse practice of these providers.

There is no doubt about the extent of public interest in alternative financial services which are perceived to be more principled and more socially useful than the conventional kind. The banking crisis of 2008 and subsequent scandals and crises in the major banks have led to a great deal of public anger and a search for anything that seems to do things differently. One example of this is the Move Your Money campaign, which seeks to persuade the public to close their accounts with the major high street banks and open new ones with 'mutually owned, community focused or ethically minded banks'.[1] It has had some success in increasing awareness of the existence of smaller and less familiar names in banking, most of which report a large increase in enquiries over the last few years.

The original intention of this study was to produce a working definition of the term 'ethical' at the outset as a guide to where to look for illuminating case studies. In practice it has proved more useful initially to consider any organisation which describes itself as 'ethical' in its own publicity and then try to analyse what it means by this. To limit the field of study by restricting it to a prior definition of what 'ethical' means would miss the most interesting and significant aspect of the study, namely the remarkable diversity of principles and practices which are described by their own promoters as 'ethical' and the widespread reluctance to offer customers clearly stated definitions of what exactly the provider regards as un-ethical. It is this lack of clarity which provides the sharpest contrast with the Islamic sector and the most instructive lesson for those attempting to position religiously inspired services within the wider ethical sector.

There is a great deal of writing and discussion in all forms of media – printed, broadcast and online – about 'ethical investing', 'socially responsible investment', 'responsible credit', 'corporate social responsibility', 'transparency in corporate governance' and 'sustainable finance', and this is not an exhaustive list of expressions indicating alternative finance and business models or at least believed to do so. Unfortunately much of this material is repetitive and derivative and does not consider the issues involved from first principles. It is full of unexamined assumptions about what is good and bad, particularly in relation to environmental issues and to the respective roles of business and of the voluntary sector. Many writers on the subject tend to quote the same sources and also each other. The term 'sustainable' is used loosely and inconsistently, often in a way which confuses financial sustainability with the environmental kind. There is some interesting work being done developing the idea that a business can only be truly sustainable in the financial sense if it promotes sustainable environmental and social practices,[2] but this has not yet found its way into much of the promotional material of the self-described 'ethical' sector. In this lack of clarity the secular ethical sector compares unfavourably with the Islamic sector, where the fundamental principles are rigorously set out and conformity with them is assessed by experts.

The Islamic sector has been one beneficiary of this widespread quest for alternatives, but in the present volatile state of public opinion there is no certainty that it will be successful in the long term in attracting and retaining interest from non-Muslims who are looking for a supposedly ethical alternative. In its current state it presents some challenges to customers from different cultural traditions and fails to satisfy some criteria which are commonly accepted as part of the wider alternative finance movement, sometimes by simple omission and sometimes because they are not compatible with Islamic principles. It has been fairly slow to take up environmental concerns and is still handicapped in this area by a perception that it is too reliant on support from Arab oil states. It cannot hope to attract much custom from non-Muslims whose liberal views on gender roles and sexuality are central to their perception of what is 'ethical'. On the other hand, the centrality of the prohibition of bank interest in the Islamic financial tradition makes practical co-operation with interest based alternative financial models very difficult, even for those Muslims who are otherwise sympathetic to the general aims of such alternatives. One of the main themes of this study is to explore what possibilities there really are for convergence between the Islamic and the non-Islamic ethical sectors.

The basic principles of Islamic finance

This book is not intended to provide a detailed guide to the principles of Islamic finance, which can be found in other books in this series, but for readers whose main interest is in the wider field of ethical finance and who are unfamiliar with the tradition of Islamic thought on finance and economics, the following brief summary may be useful.

The most important and best known principle within this tradition is the prohibition of *riba*, a term now identified with bank interest. Its basic meaning is an increase of capital through the payment of a fixed or guaranteed return. The only permissible ways to increase capital are through sale and purchase and through investment in business, where there is some risk, however theoretical, of losses.

A less well-known but equally fundamental prohibition is that of *gharar*, usually translated as speculation. This covers a spectrum from outright gambling, which is strictly forbidden in Islam, to contracts which contain unacceptable elements of uncertainty. Only expert Islamic scholars can form authoritative opinions on the more subtle forms of *gharar* which may be present in contracts and financial instruments. Some lay people, particularly those from non-Muslim backgrounds, find it difficult to understand why the payment of a return is only permissible if the capital is at risk and yet gambling and speculation are forbidden. It is quite clear within Islamic law that the purchase of shares in a company and direct investment in a new venture are legitimate forms of business activity and are not gambling or speculation, and the study of this distinction is a useful corrective to the simplistic approach sometimes found among enthusiasts for ethical finance which sees all investment in equities as a form of gambling.

Underlying the technical prescriptions of *Shari'ah* is a fundamental concept of sharing risk rather than transferring it. It is this which makes Islamic finance attractive to those disillusioned by a steady stream of revelations about the ingenious methods employed by conventional banks to protect themselves against any risk of loss and oblige their clients and account holders to suffer instead. In practice the behaviour of Islamic banks has not always lived up to this ideal of a partnership in which both losses and rewards are shared, but that only makes those who are committed to the ideal more determined to see its full potential realised.

Another way of looking at this would be that the principle of mutualism is central to the Islamic tradition. This is one of the most interesting points of intersection with the secular tradition of ethical business in Britain, where mutual and co-operative models have been historically important.

Much of the overall character of Islamic finance comes from its avoidance of debt financing and preference for sale and leasing contracts rather than the structures typically used in conventional finance. This is often interpreted by practitioners as the principle that all forms of finance must be based on real assets. Again, in practice the underlying assets in these transactions are not always as straightforwardly tangible as this principle implies, but it is this probably more than any other aspect of Islamic finance which has attracted new interest to it since the banking crisis, a crisis which to many members of the general public seemed to have been caused by trying to produce money 'out of thin air'.

Mention may be briefly made of some Islamic financial structures which embody these principles. The Islamic version of insurance, *takaful*, is a mutual assurance scheme in which the risk is shared by all the members and any profit is divided among them as well. In the venture capital model known as *mudarabah*, the financier who provides the funds to the entrepreneur has to share any losses, because the work and effort of the latter is considered to be of equal value. The most common forms of home purchase finance, *murabahah* and *ijarah*, embody the use respectively of sale and purchase contracts and rental contracts as legitimate ways of gaining an increase on capital. The 'bond like' instruments of *sukuk*, which pay a return in the form of income generated, in most cases, by a piece of real estate, are the clearest expression of the principle that all finance must be based on real assets, and lack of clarity about the nature of the claim on the underlying assets has aroused scholarly concern.

Some other principles of *Shari'ah* are relevant to a consideration of the relationship between Islamic and other ethical practices. The consumption of alcohol and pork is not permitted. There is no explicit injunction against tobacco but in recent times scholars have tended to regard it as an unacceptable intoxicant. Muslim views on matters connected with sexual relationships are generally more conservative than those typical of British society as a whole.

At the most fundamental level, to be compliant with *Shari'ah*, the path of Islam, any kind of financial or business activity must be concerned to promote human development towards a religious ideal and to avoid anything that would hinder this. It must help individuals to live full, dignified and worthwhile lives, first by providing the material conditions necessary for this and then by avoiding the encouragement of any activities which tend to damage and weaken either individuals or communities. It is at this most fundamental level that there is the greatest possibility of convergence and co-operation with other forms of ethical striving, whether by those of other religious traditions or that which arises from a secular aspiration to make a better world.

An outline of Christian thought on finance

That this section is longer than the previous one on Islamic thinking may seem inappropriate in a series expressly concerned with Islamic finance. The justification for it is that the Islamic tradition is extensively described elsewhere and that those most familiar with Islam may not be familiar with the existence of a body of Christian thinking on finance. The Christian tradition is central to understanding the non-Muslim ethical sphere in the UK and the ways in which it relates to the Islamic sector. Even though the national census of 2011 found that only 59 per cent of the population were still prepared to describe themselves as Christian, the culture of the country is strongly coloured by the historical importance of the Christian churches.

Christian attitudes to money

When the Occupy the London Stock Exchange group set up camp outside St Paul's Cathedral, and the governing body of the cathedral found itself confronted with the dilemma of whether or not to support moves to evict the protesters, the situation captured the imagination of the British public and dramatised the unresolved tensions within the Christian tradition about the appropriate attitude to wealth.

A well known passage of the Gospels describes an attempt to entice Jesus to express hostility to the government which would justify his arrest by asking him whether it was religiously acceptable to pay tax to the Roman occupiers. He responded by pointing out that coins were stamped with the name and picture of the Emperor, and saying, 'Give to Caesar what belongs to Caesar, and to God what belongs to God' (Matthew 22: 21). Although in its historical context this reply seems to have been intended as strategically ambiguous, Christians down the centuries have tried to derive guidance from it on what their relationship to money and to earthly power ought to be. In the context of the dilemma faced by the clergy of St Paul's Cathedral, Caesar took the form of the Corporation of London, the secular authority responsible for the 'City', the district in which the London financial services industry is concentrated.

One response to the dichotomy implied in this passage is the millenarian strand within Christianity, that is, a rejection of all worldly concerns as irrelevant and inappropriate and an exclusive concentration on the next life or the anticipated divine transformation of this earthly one. There are a number of Gospel passages which support such a position, notably 'my kingdom is not of this world' (John 18: 36). Throughout the last 2,000 years this tendency has periodically expressed itself in outbursts of radical fervour. In the present day it finds a congenial home in the environmentalist movement, where religious apocalyptic language is easily converted into the climate change kind.

There has always been a tendency within Christianity to idealise poverty. This is an important difference from Islamic attitudes to wealth, which developed in a trading culture. Islam never developed a monastic tradition in the way that Christianity did. The orders of monks, friars and nuns were founded on an idealisation of both celibacy and poverty and in some cases of mendicancy (begging), giving a spiritual interpretation to the relationship of dependency between holy beggars and those who supported them. This strand of Christianity keeps re-appearing to complicate attempts to develop a theology about money. Elements within Christianity simply dislike all monetary relationships, even business, and dislike the financial services industry most of all. The classic Biblical reference here is the incident of Jesus driving money-changers out of the temple precinct (Matthew 21: 12). His description of them as 'robbers' suggests it was mainly their dishonesty he objected to, but it has often been taken to indicate that involvement in sordid financial services is inappropriate for Christians.

A particularly problematic Gospel text is the story traditionally known as 'the parable of the talents' (Matthew 25: 14–28). This relates the story of a man who left his three servants in charge of his business, giving them respectively five, three and one coins (a talent being a unit of currency) to take care of while he was away. The first two increased their capital by wise investments but the third hid his for safekeeping and returned only the original amount. The servants' master was delighted with the first two and angry with the third. This parable is heavily ambiguous and has confused many generations of Christians. It has often been explained as an entirely metaphorical exhortation to make the best use of our abilities. It can also be taken at face value as an endorsement of the legitimacy of lending at interest and prospering through business acumen. On the other hand it seems to contain a strong criticism of the master's behaviour. The reprimanded servant says, 'I knew that you are a hard man, harvesting where you have not sown and gathering where you have not scattered seed'. The master replies that since he knew that, he 'should have put my money on deposit with the bankers, so that when I returned I would have received it back with interest'. The story concludes with what could be taken as an entirely cynical observation on the way the world works: 'For whoever has will be given more, and they will have an abundance. Whoever does not have, even what they have will be taken from them'. Close reading of these verses suggests a condemnation of those who make money out of money rather than by productive labour and of financial practices which make the rich richer and the poor poorer, a sentiment very similar to that found in the Quran.

Christian views on charging interest

Historically the church forbad usury, and left it to the Jewish minorities of Europe, who were permitted to practise it with non-Jews but not within their own community.[3] The church's opposition to interest bearing transactions lasted through the medieval period but finally gave way under the pressure of emerging capitalism. Some Christians however have never felt entirely reconciled to usury. As recently as 1942 the then Archbishop of York, the left-leaning William Temple, was worrying about the power of financial systems based on interest to distort social priorities and create inequality. He put forward the idea, then radically innovative but now sounding rather familiar to anyone who has studied Islamic finance, that 'so soon as the interest paid on any investment is equal to the sum invested, the principal should be reduced by a specified amount each year until the claim of the investor to interest or dividends was extinguished'.[4] It is interesting to note that it is the point where the principal has doubled that is felt to be the limit of acceptability. The most famous Quranic injunction against the charging of interest is 'devour not *riba*, doubled and redoubled' (3: 130). Temple's proposal was never likely to be adopted by any British government.

Tawney, in his famous study of religious attitudes to capitalism, says that the feeling against usury 'survived as a sentiment long after it was repudiated as a command'

and refers to the 'innumerable fables' about usurers meeting unpleasant ends as an expression of the deeply rooted popular animosity towards money-lenders.[5] This suggests that all formal religious opposition to usury is drawing on deep wells of innate resentment. Arguably the wave of popular hostility to banks following the crisis of 2008 is just the latest expression of this fundamental folk sentiment against bankers, usurers and anyone who seems to profit from other people's poverty. In this present context it is natural for Christians as well as Muslims to re-examine their own religion's earlier condemnation of usury, and for both traditions to attract wider interest.

The social and political role of the churches

Running alongside this popular sentiment against money-lenders has always been a feeling of resentment against the wealth of the institutional church. There is an obvious contradiction between the life of an itinerant preacher presented in the Gospel story of the founder of Christianity and the considerable wealth and secular power which has been acquired by the churches over the centuries, and protests against the churches' wealth have been a recurrent feature of Christian history. A recent exponent of this popular sentiment was the caller to a radio programme who was indignant at the extensive collection of artefacts made of precious metals on display in his local cathedral and called for them all to be melted down and the proceeds given to the poor.[6] This of course overlooks the artistic and historical value of such objects and of many church buildings. All of the long established Christian denominations, and the Church of England in particular, have an obligation to protect and maintain these which they sometimes find burdensome. They also have to pay salaries and pensions to their clergy. The Church of England's investment policies are therefore of interest to a study such as this.

The Church of England also has an important constitutional role; the monarch as head of state is also head of the Church and its bishops sit in the House of Lords and thus help make the law. Contrary to popular belief they are there because of the role of the Church as a very large landowner, not as representatives of religious faith.[7] The bishops are formally described as the 'lords spiritual' as opposed to the 'lords temporal', the usual aristocratic landowners. In practice however in the present day the bishops in the Lords do see their role as being to provide a Christian perspective on the issues of the day. The only occasion in recent years when their votes have proved decisive was in the rejection of a proposal to amend the laws on gambling to permit the opening of a large casino in north-west England.[8] This reminds us that, while Christianity does not prohibit gambling entirely, as does Islam, that does not mean that Christians are unconcerned about it. (The same applies to the use of alcohol and other intoxicants.) The Church of England has produced an excellent paper on gambling drawing on Christian sources as far back as St Augustine.[9] This paper clearly explains why investing in stock markets is not the same as gambling, in distinction to some public opinion but in conformity with the principles underlying Islamic finance.

By contrast the newer Christian groups are much less encumbered with commitments to buildings and personnel and can be more nimble in responding to changing social circumstances. For example they can begin working in a deprived neighbourhood simply by renting cheap office or residential accommodation there. This is one reason why such newer groups, who are usually more evangelical (proselytising) and fundamentalist in their approach to scripture than the older ones, are becoming a significant force in social and financial activism in Britain. Among some of these groups a new financial theme has emerged, the 'prosperity gospel', the conviction that material success is a sign of God's favour, or in its crude form merely that going to church and observing Christian principles in life will lead to prosperity.

Christian attitudes to the welfare state

Jesus had a 'tax collector' as an apostle, which was considered shocking because such people were loathed by the populace. St Matthew seems to have been something more similar to what we would call a tax farmer, in effect a licensed extortionist, than to HM Revenue and Customs (HMRC), the tax collecting authority in present-day Britain. In modern times the majority view within British churches has been that it is a duty to pay secular taxes because this is the main means of wealth distribution in society. Our taxes go to pay for the welfare state, which in this perspective is regarded as a secular expression of the Christian exhortation to care for the sick, elderly and unfortunate. Historically the labour movement in the UK has had strong Christian elements, which is something that should be borne in mind by readers familiar with countries where the churches are more likely to be aligned with the right in politics.

There are however substantial differences of opinion on this issue among Christians. The Church of England bishops in the House of Lords voted against reductions in welfare benefits but were criticised for this by a former Archbishop of Canterbury, George Carey, who wrote a newspaper article arguing that they ought to have been more concerned to reduce the national budget deficit.[10] His article also criticised the way that long-term reliance on benefits puts obstacles in the way of the full development of human potential that Christians should encourage. A lively public debate on the appropriate position for churches to adopt on 'the culture of welfare dependency' ensued.

Protestant ethics and Islamic modernity

Max Weber's famous work *The Protestant Ethic and the Spirit of Capitalism* makes regular appearances in writing by Islamic economists, being cited in support of diverse and sometimes mutually exclusive positions. In most cases it seems safe to say that the writers are referencing the version of Weber's thesis that has entered popular culture, rather than engaging seriously with the original text. In this simplified version, Western capitalism was a product of the culture of Protestant Christianity. In some Muslim interpretations, this explains what is wrong with Western capitalism and demonstrates the need for an Islamic alternative.

The Protestant Ethic includes an assumption that rationalism as understood in modern capitalism never appeared in the Islamic world, which would be antipathetic to most Islamic economists. Weber himself avoids expressing this as a belief in the superiority of European culture, but most Muslims would see this as implicit. It is possible to argue that Islamic finance and the associated notion of Islamic modernity represent the Muslim world's version of the Protestant ethic and thus demonstrate the equal capacity for rationalism of the Islamic world, and it is possible to believe that everything wrong with Western capitalism today is a result of its abandoning Christianity's historical opposition to bank interest. However, it is not possible to maintain both of these positions simultaneously, since the triumph of the Protestant ethic represented the acceptance of the legitimacy of charging interest.

If, as Weber famously expressed it, rationalist modernity represents the 'disenchantment' of the world, and if the world of modern finance is the supreme expression of that disenchanted rationalism, then Islamic finance, and possibly ethical finance as a whole, could be seen as an attempt to re-enchant the world. Certainly much writing on ethical finance is coloured by a desire to make transactions less impersonal, warmer and more human, while Islamic finance represents by definition a commitment to maintaining the religious spirit which Western sociologists have in the past classified as pre-modern within the bureaucratic rationalism of modern banking.

Such a notion of Islamic modernity is a key rhetorical trope among writers on Islamic finance and economics. This usually involves a conscious rejection of the Western tradition of writing about Islam as backward and a barrier to progress, presenting it instead as intrinsically rational, global and modern, and depicting Islamic banking as the outstanding expression of this. There are now Islamic branding experts who talk about 'Muslim futurists', arguing that Muslim consumers are actually in the vanguard of current market trends.[11] There is some tension between this post-colonialist assertion of indigenous modernity and the tendency of non-Muslim ethical activists to reject modernity, or at least to refuse to grant the term positive connotations, in favour of an imagined simpler and more 'sustainable' lifestyle.

Enthusiasts for both Islamic and ethical alternatives who trouble to read *The Protestant Ethic* in detail will find it even more in tune with their vision than they might originally have thought. In the final few pages Weber makes some interesting points about the possibility of the 'iron cage' of bureaucratic modernity being replaced by new ideas and ways of doing things. He speculates that 'at the end of this tremendous development entirely new prophets may arise',[12] a prediction which Muslims could perhaps choose to interpret as having been fulfilled by a belated flowering in the West of their own faith. Weber also writes that the nineteenth-century model of ever expanding industrial capitalism will probably continue until 'the last ton of fossilised coal is burnt',[13] a sentiment which will no doubt be seized upon by environmental activists as an indication that he was a proto-Green.

It would be more productive if everyone involved in the search for Islamic and other ethical alternatives could take these thoughts as cues for a wider and better informed debate on the future of capitalism, rather than repeatedly rehearsing the clichéd version of Weber's thesis about Protestantism.

The rationale for this book

The number of organisations working in some aspect of financial services which claim to be ethical is large and bewildering, and this study has had to be highly selective in choosing which ones to discuss in detail. The selection has been guided by the theme of the study, which is the relationship between Islamic finance and the wider field of ethical finance. The distinction is not simply between an Islamic approach and an entirely secular one; this is a misleading approach in the British context. Other religious traditions are well represented in the ethical sector, notably Christianity, since the United Kingdom is a Christian majority country with a long history of social activism by churches. This study seeks to explore the similarities and differences between Islamic and Christian approaches to financial matters as well as those between both of these religious traditions and a secular but self-consciously ethical approach.

The examples chosen are of three types: explicitly Muslim, explicitly Christian, and prominent names in the non-religious field. The secular examples are chosen because they illuminate key themes of the ethical approach, illustrate the difficulty of standardising policies within this sector, seem to offer possibilities for convergence with Islamic models or present important contrasts with and difficulties for Islamic principles.

The main questions which the book asks are: what possibilities are there for convergence between Islamic financial practices and other forms of ethical practice, and, is the marketing strategy of positioning Islamic finance as a sub-set of ethical finance rather than a completely distinctive proposition appropriate or misguided?

Notes

1. www.moveyourmoney.org.uk (accessed 16 November 2012).
2. Such as the work of Tony Webb, founder of The Ethical Corporation, who writes at www.tobywebb.blogspot.com.
3. Wilson, Rodney (1997), *Economics, Ethics and Religion: Jewish, Christian and Muslim Economic Thought*, London: Palgrave Macmillan, p. 33.
4. Temple, William (1942), *Christianity and Social Order*, Harmondsworth: Penguin, p. 82.
5. Tawney, R. H. (1926), *Religion and the Rise of Capitalism*, London: John Murray, pp. 36–7.
6. *You and Yours*, broadcast on BBC Radio 4, 8 November 2011.
7. This issue was discussed in detail on *Beyond Belief*, broadcast on BBC Radio 4, 13 February 2012.
8. 'Archbishop casts crucial vote against supercasino', www.ekklesia.co.uk, 29 March 2007.
9. *Gambling or Gaming, Entertainment or Exploitation?* (2003), available at www.churchofengland.org.
10. 'My fellow bishops are wrong: fuelling the culture of welfare dependency is immoral', *Daily Mail*, 25 January 2012.

11. See the discussion of the work of Ogilvy Noor in Chapter 8, 'The Concerned Consumer'.
12. Weber, Max [1930] (1992), *The Protestant Ethic and the Spirit of Capitalism*, London: Routledge, p. 124.
13. Ibid p. 123.

CHAPTER 2

RETAIL BANKING

The majority of activity in Islamic financial services in the UK is in the area of retail banking or what is commonly referred to as 'high street' banking. The highest profile entrant into the field is the Islamic Bank of Britain, which concentrates on providing a full range of accounts to individuals, families, mosques and small businesses. Similar services are provided by the large banks which have opened Islamic windows. In order to place the debate about the relationship between Islamic banking and the wider field of 'ethical' banking in its proper context, this chapter discusses in detail a number of British banks which describe themselves as 'ethical'. Some implications presented by these examples for Islamic banking are considered at the end of the chapter.

The major banks

A link between banking and religion is sometimes regarded as being confined to the Islamic sector, but this is not the case. There are Christians seeking at the present time to express their faith through work in the financial field, and the involvement of people of faith in banking in Britain has a long history. Two of the UK's largest banks, Barclays and

Lloyds, were founded by families who were members of the Society of Friends, or Quakers. One of the reasons for the disproportionate Quaker presence in banking was the legal exclusion until the nineteenth century of religious dissenters (everybody not a member of the Church of England) from the universities and some of the professions. There were therefore certain features in common with the modern experience of Muslims as a religious minority community with close internal bonds.[1]

The Lloyd family came originally from Wales, as their name suggests, but were living in Birmingham by the time the bank of Taylors & Lloyds was founded in 1765. Sampson Lloyd built himself a house in Sparkbrook, then a rural area outside Birmingham, but now, in a historical twist pleasing to anyone interested in the tradition of ethical banking, known as an area of Muslim residential concentration. Barclays is an even older foundation. It was founded in 1690 by John Freame and Thomas Gould but eventually became known by the name of James Barclay, Freame's son-in-law. John Freame was an active member of the Society of Friends.

No discernible trace of Quaker values remains in either of these banks today and few members of the public are aware of this aspect of their history. It was brought to the attention of anyone following the proceedings in July 2012 of the Treasury select committee which interviewed Bob Diamond, former chief executive of the Barclays Group, in connection with allegations concerning manipulation of the Libor rate by Barclays.[2] John Mann, a Labour member of parliament on the committee, asked him if he was aware of the principles of the Quakers who founded the bank. Mr Diamond appeared to have difficulty answering this question. Mr Mann informed him that they were 'honesty, integrity and plain dealing'. The last is characteristic of the Society of Friends, who emphasised plainness in all aspects of life. At the time of writing Lloyds has not been directly implicated in activities blatantly incompatible with the principles of its founders.

Some Muslims have always been unhappy that the Islamic 'windows' offered by some large multinational banks are insufficiently insulated from the conventional, *haraam* activity which forms the bulk of the banks' business. Barclays does not offer any retail Islamic products and so it is not directly affected by Muslim concerns, but the Libor scandal will intensify general Muslim unhappiness about the lack of clear separation between Islamic and conventional banking. The use of Libor as a benchmark to set profit rates on Islamic products which are supposedly entirely free of *riba* has always made many in the Islamic financial services industry uneasy. That was when it was thought to be *riba* but at least honestly fixed. Now Libor is *riba* and also tainted by allegations of fraud. This will inevitably encourage moves to set purely Islamic benchmarks for profit rates.

Most of the main high street banks fail to satisfy all the demands of customers seeking secular ethical banking. Barclays, Royal Bank of Scotland and HSBC have all been attacked by 'green' activists for their involvement in financing oil extraction projects considered to be environmentally damaging.[3] Recently HSBC has had to extricate itself from a scandal over a failure to prevent its services being used to launder money by drug traffickers. At the time of writing, all of the large banks are being investigated for possible involvement in manipulating the Libor rate.[4] For non-Muslims who are heavily committed to 'ethical' banking there often appears to be no reason to support the largest banks. For Muslims who care both about *Shari'ah* compliance and about wider ethical matters, the dilemma of whether to give their money to the Islamic division of a bank which appears to satisfy their primary religious concern but not other convictions which they hold can be acute.

The Co-operative Bank

The Co-operative Bank is the only bank offering a current account to have explicitly positioned itself as 'ethical', and it is going through an exciting period of development at the present time. Before 2009 it had only ninety branches. In that year it took over the Britannia building society and thus acquired another 250 branches.[5] It is now about to take over 632 branches of Lloyds Bank. During the banking crisis of 2008 the British government pressured Lloyds into taking over HBOS, but was always concerned about the size of market share for Lloyds which resulted. The later sale of some of its branches at a discount price was a condition of the financial assistance given to the newly merged bank by the government at that time. The Co-operative was favoured by regulators because the acquisition would take it to a size where it could present a real challenge to the 'big four' banks in the UK. The completion of the deal was delayed for some time but is expected to be finalised by late 2013, the deadline set by the regulators. It will result in the Co-operative having about 1,000 branches in total, which is about 10 per cent of the 'banking network', 11 million customers (4.8 million of them acquired from Lloyds) and 7 per cent of personal current accounts in the UK.[6]

This dramatic expansion of an ethically branded bank raises many interesting possibilities. On the one hand it could extend awareness of its principles and prompt customers of rival banks to wonder why they cannot do likewise. On the other hand it may be difficult for the bank to keep to its distinctive principles as a larger company. The Co-operative Group of which the bank is one division (the others being a food retailer, a funeral arranger and an insurance provider) is in fact a co-operative, that is it does not have shareholders. A proportion of its profits are distributed to members every year, in relation to their spending with the group, in a payment which has always been known as a 'dividend' and used to enjoy popular affection as 'the Co-op divvy'. Although this has become difficult to distinguish from the loyalty rewards schemes which many other companies now run, it is still a variable payment dependent on the profits of the group rather than a fixed incentive for spending a certain amount. The corporate governance of the group is also typical of a mutual, with ordinary members from very varied backgrounds elected to the main board. There is a specialist subsidiary board for the banking division consisting of finance professionals. Financial regulators have apparently expressed concern over whether the governance practices of a mutual will be sustainable after the bank has become so much larger, but the group's chief executive is convinced that they will be.[7]

The bank gives prominence in its information material to its ethical investment policy. This was introduced in 1992 and in line with its mutual status the Co-operative Group gives members the chance to vote on which issues they care about most. All of its investment decisions are made according to ethical criteria as well as considerations of the likely return. These ethical criteria are summarised in tabular form as: the environmental impact of the company, employee impact, supplier and trading policies, risk management, board structure and executive salaries and bonuses (referred to in the narrative section of the information as '"fat cat" pay'). In addition it states that it specifically excludes investment in any companies involved in 'nuclear power generation, tobacco, armaments and pornography'.[8] (The ethical policies of the supermarket division of the Co-operative

Group are discussed in Chapter 8, 'The Concerned Consumer'.)

The Co-operative Bank offers a full range of current accounts, savings accounts, personal loans and mortgages. Since 1999 it has had an internet banking subsidiary called Smile which follows the same ethical policies. A very important aspect of ethical finance is inclusiveness, rather than simply promising the wealthy to invest their money in an ethical way. The Co-operative's Cashminder is a so-called 'basic' bank account aimed at the financially marginalised. It is a current account with no overdraft or chequebook, just a debit card and standing order facilities. The information leaflet about it says 'life is so much easier with a bank account' so it is evidently targeted at people who do not yet have an account at all. A member of staff in a branch described it as being designed for 'people who are struggling with their finances' and commented that it is very unusual for any applicant to be rejected. Despite years of chivvying by successive governments, the big banks have been reluctant to offer basic accounts to those on low incomes who are unappealing customers. It may be that it is only because it does not have shareholders that the Co-operative is able to provide a good service to customers from whom it will never make much profit.

One important and often neglected aspect of inclusiveness is the barrier to opening accounts presented by the increasingly stringent rules about the proofs of identity required, which are leading in some cases to the absurd situation where people who cannot afford to take holidays abroad are required to obtain a passport just to open a bank account. The Co-operative is unusual in that it is not a requirement to produce either a passport or a driving licence to open its most basic account. It will accept as proof of identity a letter or passbook issued by the relevant government department confirming entitlement to welfare benefits, and this is in itself a significant contribution to the accessibility of its services. Possibly because of this, the Cashminder account can only be opened in person at a branch, but many of its target customers have no desire to operate their finances online in any case. (Similarly, the Post Office, discussed below, does not always require 'photo ID'.)

The Co-operative also sells insurance products. As insurance premiums rise ever higher, the need for what might be called socially inclusive insurance is becoming more pressing. This is particularly true of motor insurance, which is compulsory in the UK. The premiums for newly qualified drivers are now so high as to be simply unaffordable for many young people. In areas with limited public transport the lack of a car contributes directly to prolonged unemployment. A not insignificant number of people who end up in court for driving without insurance have effectively been criminalised by the lack of affordable policies. Co-operative Insurance has made some contribution to addressing this problem by offering drivers aged under twenty-five a discount if they agree to have a device installed in their car to monitor their driving style and then reducing premiums for those who have shown they drive safely. It is reported that customers who take this option are typically paying less than half the average premium for their age group and are also having 20 per cent fewer accidents.[9] This seems to be an example of social concern and financial prudence by the provider being in harmony.

One criticism that could be made of the Co-operative's 'ethical' policy is that it was deliberately adopted as a form of branding, rather than having been intrinsic to the development of the bank's services from the outset. At that time such a small bank had no way of competing with the 'big four' banks except by adopting a distinctive brand image which positioned it as something quite different. This inevitably put the bank in the negative position of removing aspects of its services which did not satisfy the new ethical criteria, rather than the more positive one of conceiving banking services in a new way from the outset. Arguably the most useful service the Co-operative has performed is to exert subtle pressure on the larger banks which are in its advertising implicitly positioned as 'un-ethical'. Now that it is itself about to become much larger, it may find it more difficult to maintain this image of being more socially responsible. One problem is that it attracts a disproportionate number of less commercially attractive customers. The Co-operative used to be one of only two British banks which would accept bankrupts as customers, but it has now discontinued this policy as it felt it was being unfairly disadvantaged by it.[10] This may be an indicator of a less generous inclusivity in future.

The Post Office

The Post Office group is at present entirely owned by the government, although a consultation process is underway about converting it into a mutual organisation. (For more on mutuals, see Chapter 4, 'Mutual Associations'.) As the name suggests, its primary function is handling mail, but over time it has developed well beyond this into the main point of engagement with many government services in the UK. It also offers financial products which are somewhat neglected in most surveys of ethical finance.

The Post Office does not yet offer current accounts but it provides a wide selection of savings products, insurance, credit cards and personal loans and it has now added mortgages (home purchase loans) to its range. These products are all supplied ultimately by the Bank of Ireland. Recent crises in the Irish banking system may worry some Post Office customers, but all its products are covered by the UK deposit guarantee scheme, and the type of customers it attracts are unlikely to save more than the £85,000 which is the maximum covered by this scheme. The basic savings accounts can be opened in person at a branch and, if so desired, operated entirely by depositing and withdrawing cash at a branch. This has become increasingly important as it is no longer the case with National Savings and Investment (NS&I), for which the Post Office was traditionally the main outlet. Until recently NS&I's savings accounts could also be operated at a branch of the Post Office, but in July 2012, following the government's 'contracting out' of NS&I services, this facility was withdrawn and these accounts can now only be funded by standing order from a current account and by postal deposit of cheques. This immediately excludes people who do not have a current account, although the government-funded Money Advice Service is taking the opportunity to inform NS&I customers about how to open a so-called 'basic bank account'.

The Post Office does not explicitly position itself as ethical, beyond issuing a standard statement about 'corporate social responsibility' which covers uncontroversial commitments to working with charities, reducing its impact on the environment and respecting the diversity of its staff and customers. Its products are however particularly accessible to people likely to suffer financial exclusion, and this is one of the most fundamental aspects of ethical finance. Rather than use the 'ethical' label to attract the type of customer who goes looking for such things, it has developed a clever branding strategy around the name 'the People's Post Office' which plays on the idea that Post Office services are for ordinary people. The Post Office genuinely is much easier to access than most banks. Its own figures state that it has more branches than all banks and building societies in the UK combined, that 93 per cent of the population live within a mile of a branch and 99 per cent within three miles, and that on any given date half of the adult population and half of all small businesses have used their local branch within the previous week. These are truly impressive figures which perhaps should be more widely appreciated than they are, and present many opportunities for the development of new services.

The Post Office is responsible for paying out state pensions and welfare benefits in some circumstances; it receives applications for passports, driving licences and other important government documents, and of course it also handles mail, which means that almost everybody has to go into their local branch at some time. So there is no social stereotype of any kind attached to customers of the Post Office, which is a significant difference from any other banking outlet. Nobody need ever feel uncomfortable, unwelcome or unduly noticeable in the Post Office, whereas many lower income people do feel like that in branches of the large banks. The potential of this network to deliver basic banking provision on a mass scale is enormous. The Association of British Credit Unions Limited has recognised this and is hoping to develop a partnership with the Post Office. (Credit unions are discussed in Chapter 5, 'Debt and Credit'.) Many small branches, known as sub post offices, are located within neighbourhood shops and are run by staff who are representative of the local community. This in itself is an important factor in accessibility and has a special relevance in predominantly Muslim neighbourhoods.

Because of its government remit to provide a universal service, NS&I believed that it should offer an Islamic product, but has not yet been able to resolve the problems of *Shari'ah* compliance created by the promise that all NS&I

savings are guaranteed absolutely secure.[11] If either NS&I or the Post Office itself ever succeed in developing a *Shari'ah* compliant bank account, the Post Office will be far better placed to deliver such a service to Muslims in disadvantaged areas than any of the large banks.

Triodos Bank

Triodos is considered here as an example of a bank which treats being ethical as almost entirely synonymous with being 'green' and whose brand is focused on environmental issues, arguably to the exclusion of some other ethical considerations. Its approach is strongly campaigning, and out of all of the financial services providers considered in this book it is probably the one which most deliberately and assertively promotes itself as 'ethical'.

The Triodos Group operates in five European countries, and its headquarters are in the Netherlands. Its head office in the UK is in Bristol and it also has a business banking branch in Edinburgh. It does not have any branches offering counter services to the public. For depositing cheques Triodos customers can use branches of Royal Bank of Scotland and NatWest. Since RBS has attracted more public opprobrium than any other bank in recent years this is perhaps an unfortunate association, and it also meant that Triodos was affected by the problems which RBS experienced with its computer systems in June 2012 and could not process its payments until they were resolved. However the cost of setting up a network of branches of its own is prohibitive for a small bank such as this and offering some counter access is preferable to having to rely entirely on postal deposits, which brings its own problems.

Triodos does not offer personal current accounts or personal loans. It offers personal savings accounts and uses the funds deposited to lend to businesses and community projects which are in keeping with its principles. In essence it finances entrepreneurship, both for profit and not for profit, and it encourages savings customers to feel like active participants in this process. One of its key promotional points is that it keeps its savers informed about exactly what it does with their money and it claims that it is the only bank to publish a complete list of every client to whom it has lent money. Its other distinctive feature, according to its own publicity, is that it actively seeks out positive investment opportunities rather than merely avoiding unethical ones.

Triodos is not a mutual society, it is a for-profit company. Account holders have no voting rights in the company and cannot directly influence its business practices. Its attitude to profit seeking is not well explained. Its public communications tell us that entrepreneurialism is part of the solution to the world's problems, that there is no contradiction between the bank's social goals and making a profit. The company is not however listed on the stock exchange of any country in which it operates, as this is felt to be inappropriate for what it is trying to achieve. It does not wish to have to pursue profit at all costs to satisfy shareholders. Its shares are all held internally by the Foundation for the Administration of Triodos Bank Shares, so that the bank's 'mission and identity are protected'. Decisions are made by the Foundation 'guided by Triodos Bank's goals and mission'.[12] The Foundation consists of the holders of depository receipts in the bank. These are a form of share but are only traded internally. In September 2012 Triodos announced a new issue of depository receipts in order to raise capital. It wrote to all account holders inviting them to invest in the bank in this way. At the time of writing, this issue is still open and is advertised as a chance to 'become a co-owner' of Triodos. The minimum purchase is a single depository receipt which is priced at 76 euros, at the time of writing. Because Triodos is based in the Netherlands, the dividend on depository receipts is paid in euros, which means that investors in the UK are exposed to an exchange rate risk as well as the usual risk of capital loss.

Triodos makes a great deal of use of the word 'sustainable'.[13] Its publicity material condemns 'unsustainable banking' and praises 'sustainable businesses'. This is a good example of the ambiguity of this term as used in typical ethical consumerism discourse. It is often unclear whether it refers to being environmentally sustainable, socially sustainable or financially sustainable. These are not at all the same thing and in some cases may be in conflict. To take an obvious illustration: Northern Rock built itself a new headquarters building which was reportedly exceptionally environmentally sustainable. It had to be sold as soon as it was completed because by then the company for which it was intended was not financially sustainable.

Triodos is also fond of the word 'values', and is a founder member of the Global Alliance for Banking on Values. One could point out that everybody has values; the important question is what they are. The bank seems to have embraced this term as preferable to any more rigorous expression of belief. The annual report for 2010 included this statement: 'Sustainable capitalism has great potential but should not become an ideology, because change will not come from embracing ideologies'.[14] This dismissal of an organised belief system as the basis for reform of capitalism is an uneasy fit with religiously inspired reform movements as well as with the politically motivated activism at which it is aimed.

It is difficult to locate a clear statement of the type of businesses and community projects which qualify for the bank's support. It prefers to supply a large number of examples of schemes which it has supported towards successful outcomes and to allow readers to draw their own conclusions.

A large proportion of Triodos investment goes into renewable energy. The group has a division called Triodos Renewables which deals exclusively with this. In 2011 it was stated that 150 wind turbines had been financed by Triodos in the UK.[15] Many of the solar panels and wind turbines it has financed have been installed under the 'feed-in tariff' scheme, a government initiative to encourage the domestic generation of renewable energy by paying for the energy surplus to the household's requirements which is fed in to the National Grid. This scheme was made less generous in late 2011 after the amount paid out proved much higher than originally envisaged. In its 2010 annual report Triodos complained about the unpredictability of tax incentives for renewable energy in all of the countries in which it operates.[16] This begs the question about the definition of sustainability. Are things that are environmentally sustainable only financially sustainable if they are given government subsidies? The report does go on to argue that in the long run private business may be better placed to deliver real change than government, and to suggest that the removal of all government subsidies for any form of energy generation may be the only way to enable renewables to compete fairly.[17] The free-market philosophy which this implies is not adopted explicitly or consistently in the bank's promotional material (of which it produces a considerable amount).

There are increasing concerns about the wider ethical issues involved in the policy of the present regulators of energy companies of obliging all domestic fuel consumers to pay a premium on their bills in order to subsidise the construction of renewable energy generating capacity, particularly because large landowners are able to benefit from tax incentives to construct wind turbines. It would be interesting to see some more explicit recognition of the ethical dilemmas involved in this area moderating the bank's promotion of renewables.

Triodos is very committed to organic food and farming. 'In addition to providing a dedicated service to nearly 250 UK organic farms, we work closely with the Soil Association, helping to fund its research and taking part in conversion events to win over conventional farmers to organic methods'.[18] There is no scope for discussion on the pros and cons of organic versus conventional farming here. Triodos even organises visits for savers and investors to some of the farms their money is supporting. In principle this sounds like a fine example of relationship banking, but in practice could mean no more than a pleasant day out in the countryside for some affluent city people who can afford to pay the premium on organic food. Evidently the bank is aware that its two central areas of concern may sometimes conflict with each other. The example given by a member of staff in the Edinburgh branch to illustrate the bank's commitment to understanding fully the projects it finances was that it would not support the installation of a wind turbine on an intensive pig farm.

In 2010 Triodos decided to reduce its involvement in the 'sustainable real estate sector', because of 'market developments', which is presumably a reference to falling property prices.[19] This is clearly a real dilemma for ethical investors. Can they maintain a commitment to supporting socially beneficial projects, in this case affordable housing, if it is financially risky? Once again the lack of congruence between social and environmental sustainability and financial sustainability is apparent.

Triodos does though certainly pay attention to straightforward financial sustainability. It reports that it voluntarily performed the 'stress test' imposed on some other banks by regulatory authorities and that: 'The results confirm a strong financial position with a total capital ratio of 13.6 per cent and a Core Tier 1 ratio of 12.7 per cent after a two year stress scenario. This is more than 2.5 times higher than the minimum 5.0 per cent Core Tier 1 ratio required'. This key piece of information is included in the online 2011 annual report but not given prominence in any of the publicity material which makes so much use of the word 'sustainable' in less appropriate contexts. Triodos does not pay 'variable remuneration' or bonuses. When the bank has done well all employees of the group internationally receive a modest flat rate bonus (300 euros in 2010).

Probably the most innovative schemes supported by Triodos are community land trusts (CLTs).[20] These are schemes where community groups buy land and develop it for some socially useful purpose such as affordable housing or gardening or simply for recreation. This secures the land permanently against the possibility of commercial development on it. Interestingly the bank says that CLTs are most advanced in Scotland. The laws regarding land tenure differ between Scotland and England, and Scotland has a history of activism around archaic patterns of estate ownership which has resulted in some community buy-outs in recent years. There is perhaps a certain connection between a community land trust and a *waqf*, in that the land is intended to be devoted to charitable or socially useful purposes in perpetuity. The principle however presents a challenge to both conventional and Islamic investors, since the latter would not normally be any more enthusiastic than the former about potentially valuable land being run by a not-for-profit group and excluding outside investors. Once again there is here simply a suggestion of possible convergence between Islamic and secular ethical practices. (The subject of *waqf* in the UK is considered in Chapter 7, 'Charities'.)

Triodos gives the impression of targeting affluent and educated customers. Its newsletters and information material are printed on much better quality paper than is usual with banks and contain excellent graphics. The 2010 annual report and information booklet had thick cardboard covers and embossed titles and felt like the advertising material for a luxury brand. As this conflicted somewhat with the environmental aims of the company, the 2011 report has not been made available in paper form. The language used in all of the bank's customer communications is relatively complex, that is to say it is pitched at readers with a fairly high level of education. The bank does not appear to entertain the possibility that any of its customers or potential customers may not have access to the internet. This is the only way to obtain information about the bank, except for people who happen to live in Bristol or Edinburgh. It rarely advertises in the mass media. To find out about Triodos, someone needs to be actively searching for an ethical bank or have heard about it from like-minded social contacts. This means that its customers are, as it were, pre-committed. They seek out Triodos because they already believe in what it does; they do not have to be convinced. In that sense, they are the same as the customers of Islamic banks.

The kind of enterprises which feature prominently in the Triodos newsletters for 2011 and 2012 are those which appeal to young professional couples. They include a family-run cheese farm, a maker of organic baby clothes, and a fair-trade chocolatier. One could tentatively suggest that supporting projects of this type which combine ethics with luxury consumption is an effective way of attracting the most desirable type of customer and is therefore a sound marketing strategy, independently of any 'values' the bank may have. In March 2012 Triodos launched a Junior ISA savings account (the JISA has replaced the Child Trust

Fund as an incentive for parents to save for children). An ethical children's saving account will have a strong appeal to higher-income families.

Triodos presents a powerful illustration of the problems of reaching a general consensus on the definition of 'ethical'. This lack of a common standard is the major obstacle to growth in the ethical financial sector. Triodos has defined the term according to its own uncompromising principles and is unlikely to co-operate with any organisation which does not share them. It seems particularly unlikely to regard an Islamic bank underwritten by oil money as a fellow traveller towards the sustainable future. At the level of the individual customer, of course, British Muslims may well be sympathetic to the projects which the bank favours.

Kingdom Bank

There is now an Islamic Bank of Britain, so one wonders if a 'Christian Bank of Britain' may eventually appear. To date, Kingdom Bank is the nearest thing to this. It describes itself as 'a UK based independent Christian bank with a fifty year heritage'.[21] It derives from an original charity called Assemblies of God Property Trust, founded in 1954 by a Pentecostal pastor with the express purpose of aiding the process of 'church planting' by funding the purchase of buildings for new churches. The organisation eventually found being a charity too restrictive and so launched Kingdom Bank as a wholly-owned trading subsidiary in 2005.

The bank is approved by the Financial Services Authority (FSA) and covered by the UK deposit guarantee scheme. It donates 20 per cent of its profits to Christian charities. Its mission statement is boldly worded: 'To glorify the

Lord Jesus Christ by providing distinctive Savings, Loans, Insurance and Investment products which advance his Kingdom, changing lives'.

Kingdom Bank does not offer a full range of banking services – that is, it does not offer current accounts. The amount of initial capital needed to be able to offer current accounts is a formidable obstacle to any new entrant. The Islamic Bank of Britain is very unusual in having been able to offer full-service banking from the outset. Kingdom Bank is more like a building society in that it receives savings deposits and lends money mostly for property purchase. It offers a wide range of savings accounts for individuals, churches and charities, including ISAs, fixed-rate bonds, postal accounts and children's accounts. The bank refers to its 'competitive interest rates' but they appear to be much in line with those offered by building societies (2.5 per cent on a two-year bond at the time of writing).

The bank does not offer personal loans but it does lend to churches, charities and 'social action projects'. It describes its service as being based on a specialist knowledge of the complexities of church finances which is lacking in the large banks. Kingdom is particularly interested in helping Christian projects which have been rejected for loans by other banks because of the uncertainty of their future income. It understands that it is difficult to prove a church's income for a mortgage application when a lot of it comes from 'weekly tithes and offerings'. (Tithing is the custom of donating a fixed proportion of one's income to the church. It is discussed in more detail in Chapter 7, 'Charities'.) Representatives of the bank will always meet and pray with applicants and they are happy to see a 'vision document' rather than a more formal business plan. The calculations used in deciding whether to lend seem to be entirely pragmatic. The maximum loan to value ratio ranges on a sliding scale from 80 per cent for properties valued at up to £300,000 to 60 per cent for those valued at more than £750,000. The bank calculates the average surplus of income over expenditure of the church for the past three years and then makes suggestions about how it could reduce expenditure and increase income.

Kingdom Bank also offers insurance policies, advertised under the heading 'Christian Insurance Direct: the natural choice for churchgoers'.[22] These policies are provided in association with other companies with specialist interests in church and charity customers (notably Ecclesiastical Insurance Office). They cover home and contents insurance for individuals, buildings insurance for churches and charities, travel insurance for holidaymakers and medical insurance for missionaries. The bank's specialist knowledge is apparent in the provision of public liability insurance for events organised by churches and charities, including events held in private homes (as many worship meetings are), motor insurance for minibuses operated by such groups, and personal accident insurance for individuals engaged in voluntary work. An interesting issue raised by this is whether insurance companies think that practising Christians are a lower risk than the general public. It seems likely that people with a strong faith are less likely to ruin the fittings of their homes by holding rowdy parties, to crash their vehicles by reckless driving or damage their health by smoking and drinking. This in turn raises the question of whether Christian Insurance Direct has anything other than applicants' word for it that they are indeed committed to observing Biblical principles in their daily conduct. Some assurance comes from the fact that its policies are only available from its website and are not generally advertised, which means that potential customers are likely to have heard of them from a church contact.

Kingdom Bank describes itself as 'ethical by nature'. This is exactly the same claim as that made by the promoters of Islamic finance, that financial practice based on religious prescriptions is self-evidently ethical. The problem inevitably raised is how to interpret this claim when religious traditions which both make this claim are in disagreement. There is of course a large amount of compatibility between Islamic and Christian beliefs and practice on financial matters. The obvious exception is the issue of charging interest. Kingdom Bank is happy to advertise its 'competitive interest rates' and appears to see the ethical aspect of this as lying in the 'value for money' it offers. There is certainly a strong argument that giving customers a generous return on their savings or charging them a reasonable amount for their loans rather than retaining as much profit for the bank as possible is an ethical approach to interest for a bank which is not opposed to interest as such. Kingdom is so convinced that as a Christian bank it is 'ethical by nature' that the statement of its guiding ethical principles does not go much beyond re-stating this sentiment at greater length. Apart from some comments on treating customers fairly and with respect, from which no company would dissent, the policy document consists of statements such as 'we fulfil our calling by embracing biblical principles with integrity and accountability' and 'we manage all the resources we use wisely since everything belongs to God'.[23]

It seems likely that Christian activism in financial services will become more widespread in the near future, as new entrants learn from and build on the experience of existing providers. Kingdom Bank is little known to the general public at present but could be a name to watch.

The implications of other forms of ethical retail banking for Islamic retail banking

It will be apparent from this chapter that there are very few banks offering current (cheque) accounts branded as ethical. The barriers to entry in this market are considerable, and the Islamic Bank of Britain (IBB) is very unusual in having been able to offer a full personal banking service from the outset. It could therefore potentially attract non-Muslim customers looking for an 'ethical' current account. HSBC has recently taken the decision to discontinue its Islamic retail banking services in the UK because they were felt to be insufficiently profitable. Lloyds still offers an Islamic current account but not a secular 'ethical' one. It is possible in principle that the much greater familiarity and ease of access it offers than the IBB could enable it to attract non-Muslim customers to open an Islamic account with it because of the perceived ethical nature of Islamic banking, but this would require a targeted marketing effort, and the example of HSBC is not encouraging.

The only readily available ethical current account is that offered by the Co-operative Bank, and this is likely to be the first provider to come to mind when searching for an ethical alternative for everyday banking. It was able to introduce this service because it already had an established banking network offering a full range of products and only needed to make the changes necessary to position itself as 'ethical'. Islamic banking could use this to its own advantage by arguing that secular ethical banking is simply a form of clever branding, whereas Islamic banking is intrinsically ethical from the outset.

The promotional material of Kingdom Bank does in fact use the line 'ethical by nature', which is a claim often made by Islamic banks but not usually used in their advertising in such a direct way. Islamic banking should stress its own claim to be ethical in its very nature if it wants to attract uncommitted customers. Enthusiasts for Islamic finance should become more aware of Christian financial activism and its potential to become both an ally and a competitor. Kingdom Bank gives prominence to the fact that it pays tithes to congenial charities. Although the Islamic Bank of Britain and other Islamic providers do pay *zakat* and *sadaqah* out of their funds, the public relations potential of this has not perhaps been fully realised.

Triodos Bank reminds us that Islamic banking has been relatively slow to acknowledge environmental issues as a significant public concern, but it would be neither possible nor desirable for Islamic banking to go as far as Triodos in this respect. Islamic principles are fundamental and not subject to changes in fashion, and expressions of 'green' concerns in Islamic banking should develop out of the underlying Islamic principles rather than being added on for marketing purposes.

The main lesson which the Post Office can teach any bank is the importance of approachability and excellent customer service. If Islamic banking is serious about expanding into the non-Muslim ethical market, it needs to find ways of reaching customers in smaller towns and communities outside the traditional areas of Muslim residential concentration.

Notes

1. Some factors tending to make religious minorities successful in business are discussed in Walvin, James (1997), *The Quakers: Money and Morals*, London: John Murray. This book includes an account of the founding of Barclays and Lloyds.
2. Reported on BBC Radio 4, News at 18.00 on 4 July 2012. The

survival of Quaker influence in Barclays until the mid twentieth century was discussed in an article in the *Financial Times*: 'How the traders trumped the Quakers', 7 July 2012.

3. 'Barclays, HSBC and RBS linked to "dirty financing" for fossil fuels', *Ecologist* magazine, 14 June 2011.

4. 'Libor scandal led to creation of banking panel', *Financial Times*, 6 March 2013.

5. 'Co-operative Banking Group: credit due for following instinct rather than herd', *Financial Times*, 13 June 2012.

6. All these figures are taken from a press release issued by Co-operative Bank on 19 July 2012.

7. 'Co-op's big adventure may turn sour', *Financial Times*, 18 March 2012.

8. www.co-operativeinvestments.co.uk (accessed 29 August 2012).

9. 'Co-operative Banking Group: credit due for following instinct rather than herd', *Financial Times*, 13 June 2012.

10. 'Banks must be more prepared to help the bankrupt, says Co-op boss', *Guardian*, 18 September 2012.

11. *NS&I Sharia'a Compliant Savings Review*, June 2008, p. 5, available at www.nsandi.com/files/asset/pdf/sharia'a_savings_review.pdf (accessed on 5 March 2013).

12. *Triodos Annual Report 2011*, available on www.triodos.co.uk.

13. See for example its press release dated 5 July 2012, available on www.triodos.co.uk.

14. *Triodos Bank Annual Report 2010*, pp. 11–12.

15. *Inspiring Change 2011–12*. This is a fold-out publicity leaflet.

16. *Triodos Bank Annual Report 2010*, p. 11.

17. *Triodos Bank Annual Report 2010*, p. 11.

18. *Triodos Bank* introductory booklet, September 2010. No page numbers.

19. *Triodos Bank Annual Report 2010*, p. 30.

20. *The Colour of Money*, Autumn 2011, pp. 8–11. This publication

is a newsletter sent quarterly to all customers and supporters of Triodos.

21. www.kingdombank.co.uk.

22. www.christianinsurancedirect.co.uk.

23. www.kingdombank.co.uk/about us/statement of ethics (accessed 4 September 2012).

CHAPTER 3
INVESTMENT FUNDS

Islamic investment funds are the most common form of Islamic financial product available internationally because they are easy to set up, requiring only that screening filters are used to exclude companies engaged in *haraam* activities. Writers on this subject sometimes present the choice for the investor as being simply that between a *Shari'ah* compliant fund and one compiled without regard to any principle except maximising returns. In reality there are a considerable number of non-Islamic funds in existence which use some ethical principles to screen investments. This chapter begins with a general discussion of ethical investments and then presents detailed case studies of some funds which present particular points of interest.

Overview of the ethical investment sector

Over the last few years the *Financial Times* has printed articles reporting that ethical investment funds are out-performing conventional funds, that they are under-performing them and that they are performing about the same. It has also described ethical funds as both more and less volatile than conventional ones.[1] One reason for this confused picture is the lack of clarity about what exactly constitutes an ethical fund and the variations in what is excluded from them. The other is that the relative performance of screened funds obviously depends on how those shares excluded from them are doing. At the height of the banking crisis Islamic funds out-performed conventional ones because by definition they excluded holdings in conventional banks, which were doing very badly at the time. Some other screened funds which excluded banks also benefited from this effect. As confidence in banks begins to recover, this comparative benefit is becoming less noticeable. Some ethical funds exclude oil companies (though many do not) and since this is a volatile sector, liable to sudden crises both political and environmental, their exclusion may reduce volatility and produce relative over- and under-performance by turns. A reverse effect may be the result of the prominence of renewable energy companies in ethical portfolios. This sector has benefited from government support with resulting strong performance for investors, but if it suffers as a result of the reduction of government support it may have a disproportionate effect on ethical investment.[2]

All of the organisations involved in promoting ethical investment are keen to publicise the increase in the amount of money being held in ethical funds. At the time of writing there is reported to be about £11 billion invested in 'green and ethical' funds within the UK, which has increased from £4 billion ten years ago.[3] This is of course a tiny fraction of the total held in conventional funds. The lack of clarity about which funds qualify as 'green and ethical' makes a definitive total problematic. Some ethical finance professionals have condemned some funds as being 'run by charlatans' whose claims to ethical status are unfounded.[4] In such cases it is difficult to separate commercial rivalry from genuinely outraged principles.

A point of reference for ethical investment is the United

Nations (UN) Principles of Responsible Investment. Many institutional investors say they are signatories to these principles. The UN principles use the shorthand term ESG, which stands for 'environmental, social and governance' issues, and provide a long list of ways in which such concerns should be taken into account, but not clear definitions of what actually constitutes an ESG issue. They promote constructive engagement with companies rather than exclusion, an approach not universally endorsed by the ethical sector.

EIRIS is a charitable foundation which conducts independent research on ethical and responsible investment and encourages fund managers to become more aware of the issues involved. It has been in existence since 1993. The acronym stands for Ethical Investment Research Services but it never uses the full name. Its reports and advice are provided mostly to finance professionals but it also provides an information service for the general public called Your Ethical Money.[5] The website which is the main means of delivering this service is partly funded by Friends Provident (discussed below). EIRIS prefers to use the acronym ESG to indicate its concerns, but interestingly this term is used by EIRIS in publications for finance professionals but not in material intended for end-consumers. There seems to be some assumption that non-professionals will not understand what environmental, social and governance issues are all about, possibly because the UN reference document is certainly not designed for ready comprehension by the general public. Arguably the public would prefer a clear explanation of ESG concerns to the confusingly loose and inconsistent use of the terms 'ethical', 'sustainable' and 'socially responsible' which dominates this sector.

The UK Sustainable Investment and Finance Association

(UKSIF) is a membership organisation which promotes 'sustainable and responsible' financial services. It states that it 'regards its members as its primary stakeholders' but also recognises 'a wider responsibility to civil society, in the UK and internationally, and to the environment and future generations'.[6] It has also been unable to resist the prevailing trend for describing itself as 'values-led', the essential meaninglessness of this phrase being particularly apparent when used by an organisation whose members have in fact an enormous diversity of 'values'. All of the well-known providers branded as ethical or green are members, but so are many mainstream financial services providers. Barclays, HSBC, Lloyds and Standard Chartered banks are all members, and so is the Bank of London and the Middle East, an Islamic bank. No other Islamic banks are members and no building societies belong to it except Ecology Building Society.

Probably because of the range of its membership, UKSIF has a rather circumspect approach to campaigning. Its policy is to publicise good practice but not bad, to inspire emulation of positive example rather than to condemn failure. It believes that change should be achieved mostly by voluntary effort, with legal compulsion as a last resort, and that individual choice by customers and the consequent operation of the market is the main mechanism by which change is implemented. In this it is very different from the more radical type of ethical and green activism, which emphasises the investigation and exposure of bad practice and is often suspicious of or impatient with market mechanisms.

UKSIF holds a National Ethical Investment Week every year in October.[7] This targets financial advisers as well as members of the general public to increase awareness of 'green and ethical options' in investment. It is questionable how much it succeeds in this aim rather than in simply reinforcing the convictions of those already aware of and involved with ethical investments.

Some common concerns

The discussions of individual investment strategies below will demonstrate some of the contradictions and dilemmas involved in an ethical investment strategy, but a few examples of problematic matters may be included in this introduction.

During the last few years the subject of corporate governance has become more important for ethical or socially conscious investors. The experience of the banking crisis raised questions in the minds of many investors about how much poor management and poor systems of accountability were to blame for the banks' problems getting so out of hand. A succession of highly publicised corporate crises and scandals has led to increased attempts to predict and prevent problems. Most ethical investment policy statements now list 'transparency' in corporate governance and reporting as something they expect of companies in which they choose to invest.

Shareholder activism is now becoming a fashionable idea. Attention is turning from simply avoiding companies involved in activities which are regarded with disfavour to trying to influence companies to improve their standards and to think more about how they can make their work socially beneficial. This is particularly true of large institutional investors who are increasingly aware that the size of their holdings gives them significant influence over companies' behaviour. However, such an approach has by no means been generally accepted by individual activists interested in ethical finance, who often prefer avoidance tactics.

Both Islamic and secular ethical investors like to

emphasise the importance of investing in activities which supply the basic necessities of life rather than frivolous luxuries. Both farmland and social housing seem to fit well with such an approach, yet both present ethical difficulties. There are increasing concerns about speculative purchases of agricultural land motivated by the belief that population growth will inevitably raise the price of both food and the land on which it is produced. This is true both of large-scale purchases of land in Africa by foreign investors and of small opportunistic investments in farmland in the UK. When does investment in the production of the basic necessities of life become speculation on rising food prices and an undesirable concentration of ownership of the means of production of food? In response to such concerns, principles of responsible investment in agricultural land are now being formulated. Similarly, housing is always a favoured investment by both Islamic and secular ethical investors, because property is regarded as a solid 'real asset' and housing is a basic human need. Financing social housing seems to add a positive community impact to this. But what happens if a housing association defaults on a debt secured against its property portfolio and the tenants discover that overnight an investment fund has become their landlord? Would a mutual or co-operative structure for the housing development not be preferable in terms of social sustainability, even if it deprives outside investors of an option for their ethical holdings?

The area of medical research presents some of the most difficult and disputed issues in ethical investment. The Islamic Bank of Britain now lists drug companies as one of the areas it excludes from its investments.[8] There are several reasons why this might be. Some secular activists are hostile to drug companies because of the use of animals for testing new products or because they believe that 'big pharma' encourages the over-prescription of drugs or keeps their prices too high. Some investors with religiously based exclusion policies avoid companies which sell drugs used to induce abortion or which are involved in research on stem cells.

There is no consensus on the issue of embryonic stem cell research among either Christians or Muslims. Some feel that the obligation to find effective treatments for serious illnesses and disabilities outweighs any scruples about using embryonic cells for research. Others take the view that the embryo is a complete human being from conception and that therefore research which involves destroying embryos can never be justified. The writer has met one young Muslim who takes every opportunity to argue against Islamic scholars who hold the latter view because of the presence in his family of a hereditary illness for which a cure could potentially be found by this type of research. Some British participants in this debate may be surprised to discover that Iran has an advanced programme of stem cell research, 'with the Supreme Leader's blessing',[9] relying on the fact that traditionally in Islamic law a foetus is not considered a person until the end of the first trimester. Liberal interpretations of *Shari'ah* are not commonly associated with Iran, but in fact this view of the legal tradition is more liberal than that of many British Muslims who share the Roman Catholic position of absolute opposition to any destruction of a foetus. There is of course an economic driver for permissive attitudes to medical and scientific research by Iran's many highly educated graduates.

Friends Stewardship Fund

Friends Life was, as the name suggests, founded by members of the Society of Friends, or Quakers. It was originally formed as a life assurance institution under the name of Friends Provident in 1832 in West Yorkshire. Unlike some other financial services companies with Quaker origins it has retained both an acknowledgement of them in its name and some residue of concern for the Society's values. It launched the Stewardship range of funds in 1984. These were the first investment funds in the UK to be explicitly promoted as 'ethical'. The Stewardship brand covers a range of funds for different purposes with varying investment strategies and risk profiles but all covered by the same ethical criteria.

The policies adopted in deciding which companies are acceptable for investment are detailed in a seventy-three page document available on the Friends Life website. It must be doubtful whether all customers or potential customers take the trouble to read this in full. A summary version is provided on the main information page. Stewardship uses a wide range of positive criteria for investment, that is it seeks to identify activities which should be encouraged and supported, as well as negative ones to target for exclusion. The positive criteria are listed as: supplying the basic necessities of life; offering product choices for ethical and sustainable lifestyles, for example, fair trade and organic; improving quality of life through the responsible use of new technologies; good environmental management; actively addressing climate change, for example, renewable energy and energy efficiency; promotion and protection of human rights; good employment practices; positive impact on local communities; good relations with customers and suppliers; effective anti-corruption controls; transparent communication. Negative criteria are listed as: tobacco production; alcohol production; gambling; pornography or violent material; manufacture and sale of weapons; unnecessary exploitation of animals; nuclear power generation; poor environmental practices; human rights abuses; poor relations with employees, customers or suppliers.[10] Much of this is common to all products branded as ethical and there is not space here to examine every point in detail. A few key areas of comparison suggest themselves for discussion.

The modish word 'sustainable' makes a predictable appearance second from the top in the list of positives, used as almost synonymous with 'ethical'. Once again we see organic farming and fair trade being presented as self-evident goods. The complexities of such a position are considered in Chapter 8, 'The Concerned Consumer'. In the wider areas of animal welfare, Stewardship excludes companies with more than 3 per cent of turnover derived from the fur trade and those involved in livestock production which do not have a satisfactory policy on the treatment of their animals. The policy statement discusses the issue of the testing of products on animals in some detail and has the honesty to conclude that no ethical fund can claim that its investments are entirely free from animal testing, but that this one will only invest in manufacturers of cosmetics and toiletries who also sell 'animal test free' ranges. This gives some indication of the consumption orientation of its target customers.

The Stewardship filter excludes companies which derive more than 10 per cent of turnover from the sale of tobacco or gambling activities and those with any involvement in the production of tobacco. In the case of alcohol, it excludes hotel and restaurant chains which derive more than a third of their turnover from the sale of alcoholic drinks, those companies in other areas of business which derive more than 10 per cent of turnover from alcohol and companies with any involvement in the production of alcohol. This makes Stewardship more liberal than Islamic funds, which normally have a cut-off point of 5 per cent of revenue for these three vices, but less generous than the Church of

England (considered below) which is at present prepared to allow 25 per cent. Stewardship's stance on the arms industry is straightforward: it will not invest in any companies which manufacture weapons and will review those which are not classed as being in the defence sector but nevertheless manufacture products used by the military. This reflects the Quaker origins of Stewardship: members of the Society of Friends refuse to serve in the armed forces.

The phrase 'actively addressing climate change' is carefully chosen to avoid suggesting a blanket ban on companies involved in conventional energy generation, since the Stewardship fund criteria do not include such a ban. In summary, the policy statement says that they recognise that society depends on fossil fuels such as oil and gas and that these bring economic benefits, but that they also cause much environmental damage and contribute to climate change. Therefore Stewardship will only invest in companies which are taking steps to minimise the damage they cause and to reduce their carbon emissions. The detailed implications of this for different industries are set out with admirable thoroughness.[11] Such a policy of active engagement does not though meet with the approval of all 'green' investors. The *Ecologist* magazine once reported on investors 'discovering to their horror in recent years that their "ethical" funds invest in oil', among other things the magazine considered undesirable,[12] which sounds like a reaction from customers who did not get further than the summary version of the screening criteria. The question of what policy an ethical investor should adopt to the oil industry has a particular sensitivity for those seeking a convergence with the Islamic sector, because of the importance of the extractive economies of the Gulf in the Islamic financial services industry. For those who desire such convergence, the only feasible policy is one of active engagement with the extractive industries in order to encourage them gradually to mitigate their environmental impact, and arguably this is also, *pace* the *Ecologist* and other 'deep green' investors, more likely to bring about such mitigation then a total shunning of these industries, which gives them no incentive to improve.

When first founded in 1984 the Stewardship range of funds excluded all financial services. The policy statement explains that this was because at that time the avoidance of companies considered to be supporting the apartheid regime in South Africa was one of the main concerns of ethical investors and that such investors felt that all banks were compromised over this issue. In the light of enormous changes in the world of banking since then, Friends Life reviewed the policy in 2007 and decided that 'certain financial sector companies do make a positive contribution to society' and could therefore be supported.[13] A very detailed discussion of what sort of financial services providers should be encouraged follows. The gist is that they should promote the financial inclusion of disadvantaged neighbourhoods and individuals, have high standards of corporate governance and transparency and follow good environmental practice. This has displeased some activists. In the same article cited above the *Ecologist* commented adversely on Friends Stewardship having 'relaxed its strict ethical policy to include banks such as Barclays and HSBC', appearing to imply that these banks were self-evidently unethical. Ethical investors who share this view might be interested in Islamic funds, which by definition exclude shares in conventional banks.

An unusual and noteworthy exclusion on the Friends Stewardship list is advertising agencies. Stewardship operates a complete bar on investment in the advertising industry, on the grounds that agencies will inevitably be promoting goods and services which do not conform to its other criteria. Such an attitude to advertising has implications in relation to the wider 'ethical consumer' and 'Islamic branding' movements.

Triodos Funds

Triodos has already been discussed in Chapter 2, 'Retail Banking'. Its investment funds are now considered here. The justification for this relatively extensive treatment of Triodos is that it is one of the highest profile financial services companies branded as ethical, with an active promotional campaign across both print and online media, and is persistent and unapologetic in defining ethical on its own terms. A particular point of interest in the recent launch of its 'socially responsible' investment funds is that the publicity material includes an attempt to explore the difference between 'ethical' and 'socially responsible'.

Triodos Socially Responsible Investment Funds were introduced in the UK in September 2012, although they had been available in the company's home country of the Netherlands for some time before then. There are two funds, called the Sustainable Pioneer fund and the Sustainable Equity fund. The Sustainable Equity fund invests in larger listed companies and invites the investor to 'help drive positive change in the corporate world'. The Sustainable Pioneer fund invests in small and medium-sized listed companies which are 'doing innovative things', 'pioneers in their various fields, working to bring about the change we need to safeguard our future and that of the planet'. The minimum investment in both funds is £1,000.[14]

These funds are therefore a notable example of the trend actively to seek out and support companies involved in preferred fields rather than simply avoiding those involved in fields regarded unfavourably. Instead of just saying this in a straightforward way, however, Triodos produced a long and dense article in its newsletter endeavouring to explain the difference between 'socially responsible', 'sustainable' and 'ethical'.

> Socially responsible investment (SRI) funds invest in stock exchange listed companies, balancing the social and environmental impact of the investment with the investor's financial return. In terms of scale, it dwarfs sustainable banking. In the UK alone, SRI funds assets under management were £938.9 billion at the end of 2009, according to the latest figures available. By comparison, the entire ethical banking market in the UK was estimated at just over £20 billion at the end of 2010.[15]

The term 'sustainable' is here used as synonymous with 'ethical' and both of them are opposed to 'socially responsible'. So the decision to use the word 'sustainable' in the names of both the Triodos SRI funds is very confusing, and the option to invest in either or both of these funds through an Ethical Stocks and Shares ISA is even more so. It is not at all certain that the distinction between SRI and ethical is sufficiently well defined to justify such precise figures as those given here. The 'ethical banking market' is largely defined by its own marketing terminology, but Triodos does not seem here to be defining these sectors simply by their branding but to be suggesting there is a real difference in fundamentals. Many readers of this article are likely to become more rather than less confused about what, if anything, this variable terminology really means.

Later in the article it is explained that the negative

screening criteria for these funds mean that 'companies with inherently unsustainable activities – for instance companies deriving direct revenue from weapons, nuclear energy or oil from tar sands' are excluded. It is not immediately obvious why any of these activities are unsustainable in any precise financial or scientific sense, and this is a clear example of how the term 'unsustainable' is increasingly being used to mean little more than 'disliked by environmentalists and those with certain political convictions'.

For those potential investors who persevere with reading all of the promotional material for the new Triodos SRI funds, there are some interesting and well reasoned justifications for the bank's investment strategy. The bank recognises that some of its more purist supporters disapprove of the whole idea of buying shares. 'As a sustainable bank, should Triodos be involved with stock-listed multinational companies at all?'[16] It explains that companies which are already wholly 'ethical' are not that numerous, whereas many companies are trying to be more ethical (or sustainable or socially responsible) and so by investing in them, people can influence them to continue in the right direction. Furthermore, a small change in the practices of a large company has more impact than faultless practices by a small company. Triodos presents the clothing company H&M as a specific example of this. Its clothes are manufactured in 'developing countries where labour standards are notoriously low' but it tries to 'improve the situation of workers and its impact on the environment' and is 'transparent' about any problems or accusations it faces and how it has tried to deal with them.[17] Because of this Triodos is happy to invest in H&M. This is a sensible and worthwhile approach to ethical investment, and it might be easier to decide whether to trust Triodos with one's money if such reasoning was given greater prominence.

Ecclesiastical Funds

Ecclesiastical was one of the sponsors of National Ethical Investment Week 2012, which may be an attempt to increase awareness of its services outside the religious field which is its specialism. Ecclesiastical Insurance was founded in the late nineteenth century to provide insurance to Anglican churches and still does provide insurance for 95 per cent of them. It has now expanded this specialism to provide insurance for Catholic churches and for synagogues, mosques, Hindu temples and Sikh gurdwaras. It describes this field of activity as 'faith insurance', which could be a puzzling term to anyone not aware that it refers to buildings. The company's work in providing a full range of insurance services for faith groups was referred to in connection with Kingdom Bank in Chapter 2, 'Retail Banking'. In addition Ecclesiastical now offers specialist insurance services for charities, educational establishments, residential care homes and 'heritage and period properties'. This last appears to have developed out of the company's original specialism in Anglican churches, the majority of which are old, sometimes very old, and of historical and architectural importance. Ecclesiastical is now, it says, the leading insurer of Grade 1 listed buildings in England.[18] The company also provides the usual range of home insurance to individuals.

Under the name Ecclesiastical Investment Management Limited another branch of the company provides investment funds, bearing the brand name Amity, which are promoted as ethical. (It also offers two non-screened funds which are not branded as Amity.) These were founded in 1988 and Ecclesiastical claims that this makes it one of the earliest providers of 'socially responsible/ethical' investments. What is more, the same manager has been in charge of Amity funds ever since their foundation, which is very unusual.

It describes its investment strategy as beginning by choosing companies with a potential to generate strong returns and then screening their activities. The negative screening factors, that is the activities excluded, are involvement in alcohol, tobacco, gambling, pornography, strategic weapons production, and the use of animals to test cosmetics or household products (the testing of pharmaceuticals on animals is acceptable but the finding of alternatives is encouraged). This is very similar to the negative screening criteria still typical of most Islamic investment managers. Amity does though have a long list of positive screening factors which it aims to seek out and encourage, which can be summarised as: high standards of corporate governance, treating customers fairly, respect for human rights and the environment, and working to improve the living standards of workers and their communities. With regard to 'oppressive regimes' the policy is to consider each case individually and to distinguish between 'activities which benefit people and those which benefit the regime'.

The details provided by Ecclesiastical are rather brief compared with those of most companies which apply ethical screening. Presumably the experience accumulated by a head of investments who has been in post for over twenty years makes it much easier to apply a consistent Amity approach without the need to spell everything out. It is also likely that the strong faith-based image and brand loyalty which the company has built up through its work with churches means that customers trust it to adhere to their own principles, particularly if these are based on Christian beliefs.

Church of England Investments Group

The rest of this chapter has been concerned with investment options for individuals, but the final example studied is of the ethical policies of an institutional investor. The Church of England is, for historical reasons, the possessor of substantial wealth, reportedly in the region of £8 billion.[19] It relies on investing this profitably to fund the salaries and pensions of its clergy, but as a Christian body it naturally wishes to invest in an ethical manner. There is also a public relations issue involved, since the importance of the Church in the national life means that its investment policy receives much more scrutiny than that of smaller churches and other religious bodies. The Church expresses this as 'being mindful of the need to avoid undermining the credibility, effectiveness and unity of the Church's witness by profiting from, or providing capital to, activities that are materially inconsistent with Christian values'.[20] It has had an ethical policy in place since it first began to engage in equity investments in 1948. The Church's Ethical Investment Advisory Group (EIAG) carries out research on possible investments and advises the church personnel who make the final decisions on investment. The policy statements issued by the EIAG, which are all easily accessible on its website,[21] form a useful case study for this book, partly because of the prominence of the Church of England and the sheer size of its holdings, and partly because the group's position statements are formulated with a clarity and thoroughness which some other bodies would do well to emulate.

Policies have been developed to cover the following areas: responsible employment practices, best corporate governance practice, conscientiousness with regard to human rights, sustainable environmental practice and sensitivity towards the communities in which business operates. The

EIAG explicitly pursues a policy of constructive engagement with the companies in which it does invest, seeking to use its influence as a substantial shareholder to encourage companies to improve their practice in these five areas. In some cases it holds discussions with representatives of companies which it is not yet prepared to recommend for investment about how they could make changes which would make them acceptable to the Church. It has recently written to more than 200 UK companies expressing concern about excessive executive remuneration, and twenty-two of these companies were prepared to meet with EIAG representatives to discuss the issue.[22] It will only disinvest completely if a company fails to respond satisfactorily to its concerns. In this it is very much in line with the general trend towards more positive ethical investment policies which actively seek to improve matters rather than the more passive approach of the past whereby investors felt they had done enough if they merely avoided unacceptable companies. For example, at the present time the Church 'is engaging with BP about operational safety',[23] presumably as a consequence of the disastrous failure of one of BP's oil rigs in 2010 which killed a number of its personnel and caused enormous environmental damage. Some activists were so disgusted by this incident that they now campaign against any involvement with BP or in some cases with oil companies generally. It is open to debate which approach will be more productive in the long run.

Companies excluded altogether from investment are those which derive more than 3 per cent of their revenues from pornography and those which derive more than 25 per cent of turnover from tobacco, gambling, high interest rate lending or human embryonic cloning. The EIAG does not at present exclude completely companies working on embryonic stem cell research (unlike the apparent position of the Islamic Bank of Britain) but is adopting the policy of active engagement with them. It recognises the potential of such research for advances in the treatment of serious medical conditions but seeks to ensure that it is only used when there is no other option. It also recognises that there is a variety of sincerely held opinions among Christians on the status of the human embryo. The current statement of policy in this area is dated 2008 and an updated one is in the course of preparation. With regard to the arms industry, EIAG recommends avoidance of investment in companies with more than 10 per cent of turnover derived from conventional weapons and those with any involvement at all in 'indiscriminate weaponry'. The EIAG has used the long tradition of Christian thinking on what constitutes a 'just war' to develop this distinction between different types of armaments.

The presence in the list of exclusions of high interest lending is significant, as it demonstrates that while Christians are not forbidden to be involved in any kind of lending at interest, the Church does recognise that some forms of *riba* are ethically dubious. The EIAG has been monitoring the type of recent developments in the field of high interest lending which are discussed in Chapter 5 of this book, 'Debt and Credit'. Similarly, while the Church of England does not forbid its members the use of small-scale forms of gambling such as raffles (while Islam and some other Christian groups do) it is very aware that gambling is the cause of many social problems. Its review paper on gambling acknowledges the diversity of opinion within the Christian churches and within the voluntary sector generally on whether or not to accept funds raised by the National Lottery, which this paper argues has made gambling more socially acceptable and reduced direct donations to charities.

The policy of the Church on alcohol is relatively complex.

At present it excludes investment in any companies deriving more than 25 per cent of turnover from the production or sale of alcoholic drinks. The EIAG is working on developing specified minimum standards of corporate responsibility in alcohol retailing, and intends that in future it will only retain a ceiling of 25 per cent as acceptable for investment if the company has met these standards. Companies involved in the production or sale of alcohol which have failed to meet these standards or have not yet been investigated will have a ceiling of 5 per cent of turnover for investment. The group feels that the relatively high percentage permitted in the past does not adequately address the present phenomenon of supermarket chains and other very large retailers whose sales of alcohol are high in absolute terms yet not as a percentage of their total turnover.[24]

While some Christian groups do regard any consumption of intoxicants, including alcohol, as unacceptable, the Church of England has always permitted moderate consumption of alcoholic drinks, and believes that its investment policy in this area must reflect this. There are also difficulties arising from the ritual use of wine in the Eucharist, which makes it awkward to argue that the use of wine is intrinsically displeasing to God.[25]

The recently retired chair of the EIAG, John Reynolds, had an unusual combination of expertise in that he obtained a degree in theology and then became an investment banker. He contributed a thoughtful paper to the collection of responses to the banking crisis edited by the Archbishop of Canterbury.[26] It stands out from much writing about money by Christian thinkers in its lack of any reflexive distaste for the financial markets as a whole. Rather it considers in detail exactly which aspects of the behaviour of investment banks could be regarded as unethical. Interestingly, he cannot see any intrinsic objection to short-selling, which is regarded as

haraam by most Islamic scholars and attracted much condemnation from the general public during the crisis. At the
beginning of 2012 Mr Reynolds was succeeded as chair of the
advisory group by James Featherby, who also studied theology at university before embarking on a career as a corporate finance lawyer. The announcement of his appointment
mentioned a number of Christian organisations in which he
was active and said that he had 'thought deeply' about issues
of business ethics. The Church of England is fortunate to
be able to recruit people with both high-level expertise in
finance and a strong religious faith, and their work provides
a valuable reminder that this combination is not unique to
Islam.

The implications of other ethical investment policies for Islamic investment funds

Perhaps the most important lesson to be learned from a
detailed consideration of the policies of non-Islamic ethical investment managers is that the variability in such policies can be a source of great confusion to potential clients.
The great strength of Islamic financial services is that they
adhere to principles which are clearly set out, generally
understood and monitored by expert scholars. The commonest complaint among those working in secular ethical
investments is that the lack of standardisation of screening
criteria increases the cost of developing and managing such
funds and makes promotional work more difficult. While
Islamic finance rightly seeks to position itself as one form
of ethical finance, it will never be able to align its principles exactly with those followed by other ethical providers,
and it should not become distracted by trying to do so. The
Church of England has developed policies of great detail
and subtlety based on its fundamental Christian principles

and applies them with close attention to present social conditions in Britain. This is a better example for Islamic finance in Britain to follow than 'ethical' policies which are not just applied to but based on more transient concerns. What Islamic providers would do well to emulate though is the responsiveness to public concerns and the effort made to keep customers informed and included in decision-making which the most successful secular ethical providers display.

Notes

1. One article which acknowledged the scale of fluctuation in relative performance was 'Why green investing remains in the shade', *Financial Times*, 22 October 2012.
2. This point about concentration of risk in ethical portfolios was made in 'Going green may not be to all tastes', *Financial Times*, 31 July 1012.
3. EIRIS press release dated 15 October 2012, available on www.eiris.org.
4. 'Green funds: an ethical dilemma', *Financial Times*, 2 December 2010.
5. The EIRIS website is www.eiris.org. Your Ethical Money is at www.yourethicalmoney.org and can also be reached from the EIRIS site by clicking 'For consumers'.
6. All of this information is taken from www.uksif.org/about (accessed on 28 October 2012).
7. This has a website all year round: www.neiw.org.
8. www.islamic-bank.com/personal-banking (accessed on 4 October 2012).
9. Nasr, Vali (2009), *The Rise of Islamic Capitalism*, New York: Free Press, p. 7. (This book was previously published under the title *Forces of Fortune*.)
10. www.friendslife.co.uk/sri, then click on 'Customer' section (accessed on 9 October 2012).

11. *Stewardship Criteria and Policies*, pp. 26–30. Downloadable from www.friendslife.co.uk.

12. 'Ecologist guide to ethical investments', *The Ecologist*, 5 November 2010.

13. *Stewardship Criteria and Policies*, p. 19.

14. *An Invitation to Help Build a Better Future*, a promotional booklet issued by Triodos in September 2012. Pages are not numbered.

15. 'Socially conscious investment' in the Triodos newsletter *The Colour of Money*, Autumn 2012, p. 9.

16. 'Socially conscious investment', p. 9.

17. *An Invitation to Help Build a Better Future*.

18. www.ecclesiastical.com (accessed on 24 October 2012). The designation 'Grade 1 listed' means that a building is recognised as being of prime historical or architectural importance.

19. Mason, Edward, *The Church as Institutional Investor*, June 2011, posted on the website of the St Paul's Institute, www.stpaulsinstitute.org.uk. The author is Secretary of the Church of England Ethical Investment Advisory Group, described below.

20. Church of England Ethical Investment Advisory Group, *Statement of Ethical Investment Policy*, November 2011. This is available on www.churchofengland.org/about-us/structure/eiag.aspx.

21. www.churchofengland.org/about-us/structure/eiag/ethical-investment-policies.aspx. There is a list of links to these statements down the right side of the home page (accessed on 8 October 2012).

22. Church of England Ethical Investment Advisory Group, *Annual Report 2011/2012*, p. 4.

23. Mason, Edward, *The Church as Institutional Investor*, June 2011.

24. Church of England Ethical Investment Advisory Group, *Alcohol Investment Policy*, June 2011, p. 2.

25. These theological complexities are explored at length in *Alcohol Investment Policy* pp. 2–5.

26. Reynolds, John (2010), 'Investment banking: the inevitable triumph of incentives over ethics', in Williams, Rowan and Elliott, Larry (eds), *Crisis and Recovery: Ethics, Economics and Justice*, London: Palgrave Macmillan.

CHAPTER 4

MUTUAL ASSOCIATIONS

The principle of mutualism is one of the central elements of the Islamic financial tradition. The concept of sharing risk rather than transferring it underlies most of its precepts and structures. For this reason it is of particular interest here to examine the British tradition of mutual societies, an independently evolved ethical tradition of shared risk, co-operation and mutual support. Many financial institutions which owe their existence to this tradition are still flourishing at the present time, most notably those known as building societies. The many points of similarity between Islamic principles and this secular mutualism are a rich source of inspiration for the future development of ethical finance in the UK.

The history of mutuals

The origins of building societies lie in the small mutual aid groups which appeared in the nineteenth century for the purpose of helping their members to buy or build a house. All the members would contribute a proportion of their wages regularly to the savings pool of the society and these funds would be used to purchase houses for all the members in turn, the order in which members benefited usually being decided either by drawing lots or by consensus agreement about the members who were in greatest need. In some cases the society was wound up once all the members had a house, and these groups were known as 'terminating societies'. Other groups, known as 'permanent societies', continued in existence indefinitely to work for wider purposes of mutual benefit, and in some cases these have survived into modern times. For example, the Leeds Permanent Building Society was founded in 1848 and was well known under that name until 1995 when it merged with the society originally established as the Halifax Permanent in 1852. After shortening its name and absorbing a couple of other societies the Halifax later became one of the most prominent building societies to demutualise, with consequences considered below.

It can be seen that these societies had close similarities with the savings groups often formed by first-generation immigrants to the UK in the 1950s and 1960s for the same purposes (often called *kameti* groups in their Pakistani version), and it is easy to understand how such a useful practice could develop independently among people of different cultural backgrounds.

An important aspect of the work of the early building societies which is not widely understood was that in an age when the right to vote was based on ownership of property the object of funding house purchase was not simply to provide the members with somewhere decent to live but to qualify them for the franchise. This was one reason why some societies became 'permanent', because once the members had gained the vote through property ownership they sometimes wished to work together for wider political and social change.[1]

Because of their very limited and local fields of operation there was originally a very large number of building societies. In 1900 there were 2,286. This number has now been greatly reduced, mostly by mergers to form larger societies, and at the present time there are forty-seven building societies in the UK, employing 42,000 staff and serving 25 million customers. There are enormous discrepancies in size and the figures as a whole are skewed by the fact that the largest society, Nationwide, has 60 per cent of the sector by assets, and is referred to in the recent Treasury report on the future of the sector as a 'big, systemic institution' which should be included in any review of the future of banks.[2] The second largest building society, the Yorkshire, has only 13 per cent of the sector by assets, and some societies are still very small by modern standards. All societies are jointly owned by their members and have no external shareholders. All members are entitled to vote at annual general meetings.

The Building Societies Act 1986 mandates that at least 50 per cent of the funds of any financial institution calling itself a building society must be obtained from deposits by its members and no more than 50 per cent from the wholesale money markets. At least 75 per cent of its lending must be secured on residential property.[3] In addition there are restrictions on the use of some higher-risk financial instruments such as derivatives and on foreign exchange transactions. This means that the business model of building societies is intrinsically lower risk than that of banks. Because their capital to lending ratios are already more stable than those of the banks, building societies have had no difficulty in meeting new regulatory requirements in this area. The government has recognised this and decided to exempt building societies from the new requirements for banks, in order to avoid their having to satisfy two different and overlapping sets of regulations.[4] At the time of writing, the Treasury is undertaking a separate consultation on the future of building societies, with a view to promoting their distinctive contribution and removing any possible obstacles to this, whilst not inappropriately relaxing the restrictions which have made them more stable.

Lending by building societies for home purchase has held up much better than lending by banks during the last few difficult years. In the first five months of 2012 it was 40 per cent higher than the same period in 2011, while the banks' lending was only 4 per cent higher.[5] Because of this differential the market share of building societies has increased. In July 2012 they had 24 per cent of the mortgage market in the UK and held 22 per cent of personal savings.[6] The Building Societies Association likes to draw attention to the higher standard of customer service it believes to be found among its members, and this appears to be borne out by the figures. Only 3.5 per cent of complaints to the UK's financial ombudsman were about building societies, which is much lower than their market share.[7]

Until the 1980s building societies were the only institutions permitted to provide residential mortgages but as part of a general trend to deregulate financial services at that time banks were authorised to offer them as well and subsequently became dominant in the mortgage sector. As banks came to seem more exciting during this period, some building societies became impatient with the restrictions on their ability to borrow, which limited the expansion they desired, and they therefore chose to demutualise and convert to banks. The first to do so was Abbey National in 1989 and the last was Bradford & Bingley in 2000. Of the ten societies which demutualised during this period none has survived as an independent bank[8]. All of them have been taken over by other companies and some of them have required government assistance.[9]

Because of the mutual status of building societies, a general vote of all members was necessary to agree conversion to a bank. All members received shares in the new bank which were often worth thousands of pounds and this meant that they had a direct financial incentive to vote for demutualisation. This led some members of other societies to campaign for demutualisation, indeed in some cases to open accounts with multiple societies in the hope of receiving payments from all of them on conversion, and for a time the very survival of the principle of mutualism seemed to be in jeopardy. To protect their mutual status, some societies introduced a requirement for new members to sign a statement waiving their right to receive shares in the event of demutualisation. The trend has now moved in the other direction as building societies have been observed to survive the banking crisis so much better than banks.

Ecology Building Society

The Ecology Building Society is considered here as an example of a very small and specialised society. It was established in 1981 at a time when environmental issues were fashionable and much discussed and the word 'ecology' was commonly used in the same sense as the term 'green' is now. Despite initial public scepticism about its viability, it has survived and in its own terms flourished. For the first twelve years of its existence it was the smallest building society in the UK, but has now risen to number forty-two out of forty-seven by asset size.[10]

Its foundation was in the true spirit of the early mutual societies. In 1980 ten supporters contributed £500 each to provide the £5,000 which was then the minimum funding required to found a building society. (It is no longer legally possible to found one with such a small amount.) In 1981 the Ecology began trading in a 'tiny' office in a small town in

Yorkshire. It has moved only a few miles and is now based in Keighley.[11] Its assets have now reached £103 million.[12] Its net profit in 2011 was £425,000, which though tiny by the standards of other building societies, let alone banks, represents a 24 per cent increase on the previous year and is thus a cause of celebration. Its mortgage lending was £18.3 million, up from £14.5 million in 2010; its savings balance had increased by 8.5 per cent to £96.14 million; and its asset growth was up by 8.1 per cent to pass the £100 million milestone.[13]

The Ecology actively promotes itself as an example of ethical finance. Its 'mission statement' as expressed in the banner headline on its website and in its press releases is that the Society 'aims to build a greener society through ethical savings accounts, sustainable mortgages and mutual values'. It seized the opportunity presented by the Barclays scandal in June 2012, issuing a press release entitled 'Time to put ethics at the heart of financial services', in which it stated that 'the Ecology building society does not set the Libor rate and has never sold interest rate hedging products'.[14] It is unlikely that any of the financial journalists who received this statement would ever have thought that it did, since the legal restrictions on the activities of building societies preclude both of these practices, but it is a good indication that the society feels that the public mood is now on its side.

An unusual feature of the Ecology's policy on savings accounts is that, rather than confining itself to advertising its competitive interest rates, it has made a firm commitment to never paying an interest rate of below 1.00 per cent gross to savers. During the period of exceptionally low Bank of England base rates since January 2010 this commitment must have become onerous, but the society held the minimum interest paid on savings at 1.00 per cent and has recently increased its rates on some savings products.

All of its savings products are branded with 'green' sounding names, such as the Earthsaver Bond and the Eco-60 account. The society makes a donation of £1 to an overseas development charity for every £1,000 invested in the Earthsaver Bond. Its publicity emphasises that savings are being used to support projects that are both environmentally friendly and socially beneficial, and it also encourages potential savers to feel that they are becoming part of 'a community of like-minded people' rather than making an impersonal financial decision.

The Ecology offers mortgages throughout the UK, but in 2011 it lent on only 126 properties. Of these, 85 per cent were residential and the rest were 'developments for community gain'. The society's criteria for deciding which properties it is prepared to lend on show a commitment to helping to create and sustain stable communities as well as to reducing environmental impact in the ways more usually associated with the 'ecology' movement. It will not lend on properties which are intended for use as holiday homes, presumably because it is aware of the damaging effects on rural communities when a large proportion of properties are bought as second homes. With this policy it has excluded a significant amount of potential business from affluent customers who may see no distinction between rural living and 'green' living. It is opposed to non-organic farming and so will not lend for farm developments which include intensive agriculture, or riding stables. (It also excludes houseboats, caravans and homes on parks where occupancy is not permitted for the full year, but this is commonly the case with mortgage providers.)

On the other hand the Ecology looks favourably on applications for finance to fund all kinds of renovations and conversions, because these are 'a form of recycling', and to buy terraced housing because this is intrinsically energy efficient, and it funds new-build homes designed to a high standard of energy efficiency and using renewable materials. Its commitment to lending on large renovation and conversion projects is distinctive and has brought it business which other societies and banks have rejected, while its praise of terraced housing must be welcome to the millions of families who have no other option in the cities where they live. The favouring of these projects is in itself a form of social inclusiveness.

In addition to lending for individual dwellings, the Ecology will lend for premises for small and community businesses, organic farms, 'small woodlands', housing co-operatives and housing association developments. It sometimes enters into partnership arrangements with developers of social rented or 'affordable' housing which meet its standards for environmentally benign building methods, energy efficiency and promoting community cohesion. Until very recently the Ecology would not lend on buy-to-let properties, but it has now introduced a specialist mortgage for such purchases, for small-scale landlords only. Properties purchased for letting must satisfy the usual criteria of being built or converted to a high standard of sustainability, and once again renovations are favoured.

The society's commitment to reducing energy consumption and carbon emissions has led it to develop some innovative mortgage products which promote these aims, branded as the 'C-Change discount'. It offers a discount on the interest rate on a mortgage in proportion to the standard of energy efficiency achieved in the home being financed, as assessed for the Energy Performance Certificate. There are three versions of this discount: for buying or building a home already classed as an 'eco build', for retro-fitting older homes with energy saving measures, and for installing renewable energy generating equipment in existing homes. This last is described as being intended for 'small scale works to existing properties', which would appear to exclude the large wind farm developments which have aroused some controversy (as discussed in the section on Triodos in Chapter 2, 'Retail Banking'). The 'C-Change retrofit' offers a very attractive option to people who have no choice but to live in one of the highly energy inefficient older properties of which Britain still has millions, which are difficult to keep warm and produce large fuel bills in the attempt. The borrower gets a reduction in the interest rate on mortgage repayments of 0.25 per cent for every grade of improvement in efficiency; for example if the rating of the property improves from E to C they receive a reduction of 0.5 per cent. The Ecology won the Green category of the awards sponsored by *Mortgage Gazette* in 2012 for this initiative.

The concept of using variations in loan repayment rates to incentivise some form of ethical action seems to have scope for use in other contexts by other lenders, including Islamic ones. It could be used to indicate that the finance company is not interested simply in maximising profits but would like to help customers by reducing their payments, if they are prepared to co-operate in the attainment of some mutually desired outcome.

An unusual feature of the Ecology's mortgages is that they do not insist on life insurance being taken out as a condition of approval of a home loan. A statement from the society[15] expressed the belief that other lenders insist on this simply in order to make profit on the sale of the life insurance product, rather than to protect their loan, because life insurance gives security to the borrower, not the lender. The Ecology is content to rely on the repossession and sale of the property in the event of the death of the borrower. Other lenders would say that this does not protect them against a fall in the value of the property, while the drawback from the borrower's point of view is that in the event of the death of a main earner without life insurance the rest of the family might lose their home. The insistence on life insurance is a problem for some Muslim home buyers, who in addition to believing that interest payments are prohibited by *Shari'ah* also in some cases have objections to insurance and particularly to what appears to be gambling on the date of one's death, so the Ecology's approach to this matter could fruitfully be studied by other financial institutions.

In terms of inclusiveness and accessibility, there are some problems with the Ecology. Because its only premises are its headquarters in West Yorkshire, it cannot offer any face-to-face transactions. Deposits to savings accounts can only be made by posting cheques to this office, which means that Ecology savers need to have either a bank current account or an account with another building society which can issue counter cheques. Its accounts are not suitable for those who wish to save small amounts in cash. They are therefore a secondary option for people whose primary banking needs are being met elsewhere.

The remarkable success of the Ecology is an example of what can be achieved by adhering uncompromisingly to clearly defined principles. In marketing terms this translates into knowing exactly who its potential customers are and not making the mistake of alienating its core supporters by trying to appeal to the mass market. There may be lessons here for other providers which offer a distinctive service, including Islamic ones.

Yorkshire Building Society

The Yorkshire Building Society is considered here as an example of a building society which does not brand itself as ethical and yet has adopted business practices which would be generally regarded as ethical. It is the second largest society in the UK and has its headquarters in Bradford, West Yorkshire.

The frequency with which Yorkshire appears as the home county of organisations studied in this book is probably not just coincidence. The region is the heartland of the building society movement. Halifax and Leeds, which both produced notable societies, are in the same region. The Co-operative Group was born just over the border in Rochdale, Lancashire, and now has its headquarters in Manchester. This stretch of the country, including the cities of Leeds and Manchester and the towns in between them, was the birthplace of the industrial revolution and was until the mid-twentieth century the location of a very large textile industry which traded globally. It therefore naturally tended to produce a cluster of financial services to meet the needs of the new class of industrial employees. Now that the textile industry has declined and this region has been left with severe unemployment and deprivation in consequence, there are new challenges for these financial service providers to meet.

The Yorkshire is committed to retaining its head office and customer contact centre in Bradford and not moving them overseas to take advantage of lower wages, as many British companies have done. This has a particular relevance for the British Muslim community. The majority of first-generation Muslim immigrants to Yorkshire were recruited to work in the textile industry, particularly to work the night shifts for which it was difficult to recruit local labour. The decline of that industry has left large numbers of Yorkshire Muslims among the unemployed. They now find that many companies are outsourcing jobs which can be done over the phone or internet overseas, often to the countries from which their parents originally came. There is a cruel historical irony in this. The decision of a large financial services provider to remain in Bradford and offer employment to local people is therefore very welcome.

At the end of 2011 the Yorkshire Building Society Group had assets of £32,647 million which represented 13 per cent of the total assets of the building society sector.[16] In the last few years it has absorbed several other societies: the Barnsley, the Norwich and Peterborough, and the Chelsea. All of these smaller societies had run into difficulties during the years following the banking crisis of 2008 and decided that merger with a more stable society was the best solution. The Chelsea had itself recently absorbed the Catholic Building Society, a survivor of the type of specialist society which used to be common, in this case one which provided mortgages for clergymen. This reflects a long-term trend for consolidation in the building society sector. The particular advantage for the Yorkshire is that, while the original society is strongest in the north of England and Scotland, the acquisition of societies based in the south and east of England has given it nationwide coverage. This reflects another long-term trend: to decreased localism in the mutual sector.

The Yorkshire does well in the areas of minimising environmental impact, working in local communities and contributing to charities. It says that it recycles 80 per cent of waste in branches and 90 per cent at head office. It encourages all members of staff to spend two paid days a year working on voluntary projects in their local communities. It has its own charitable foundation which in 2011 donated £462,000 to causes which were mostly nominated by members of the society.[17] Its most interesting charitable initiative is the scheme named Small Change, Big Difference, whereby all holders of savings accounts are encouraged to agree that only interest payments of whole pounds should be made to their accounts and the odd pennies donated to the scheme. This generates several hundred thousand pounds every year which is given to charities and local projects nominated by members. Some Muslims who object to receiving interest payments would like to donate all of the interest on their savings accounts to charity but are usually told that this is impossible with the software presently in use. Perhaps one day the Yorkshire or some other society could adapt the Small Change scheme to allow the option of donating all the interest and not just the odd pennies.

The Yorkshire also scores highly on inclusiveness and accessibility. Its Cash Transactor account can be opened by anybody with a minimum of £1 and deposits can be made in cash at branches, but it also offers facilities to have wages paid directly into the account and to make standing order and direct debit payments, which means that account holders can benefit from the discounts available for paying household bills by direct debit. Cash withdrawals can be made by card at ATMs or in branch and although there is no cheque book, a society cheque can be issued in branch on the account. This account therefore offers all the functionality of a 'basic bank account', and the Yorkshire offered it many years before the government started trying to persuade the big banks to offer basic accounts.

The Yorkshire does not ostentatiously use any of these praiseworthy activities in its promotional material but concentrates on advertising what it regards as its competitive interest rates and high standard of customer service. This may reflect a pragmatic understanding of what is really important to customers even if they claim to be motivated by ethical considerations. On the other hand the Yorkshire may be failing to reach some potential customers who genuinely are motivated by ethical considerations.

Gentoo Genie

Gentoo is a housing developer based in Sunderland, in the north-east of England. It is not a mutual society but its Genie product is included here as a very interesting and significant example of an Islamic model of home purchase finance being developed for the general market. Natalie Elphicke, a lawyer with Stephenson Harwood, a law firm with expertise in Islamic finance, developed the legal framework of the Genie product for Gentoo and was a finalist in the award for legal innovator of the year, made by the *Financial Times* newspaper in 2011, for her work for this client. She took the diminishing *musharakah* model of property purchase which is widely used by Islamic providers and developed it in a way that made it accessible to a much wider range of purchasers. Under a diminishing *musharakah* model the customer pays instalments towards the purchase of increasing shares of equity in the property and at the same time pays rent for the use of the proportion of the equity still owned by the bank. The ratio shifts until the purchaser has completed payments for the full amount of the equity. Islamic banks which provide this type of home purchase finance require a deposit just as large as that required by a conventional mortgage provider – at least 20 per cent of the value and these days often more – and this can be an insuperable obstacle to many people on lower incomes who are unable to save up such an amount.

The version developed by Ms Elphicke for her client Gentoo does not require any deposit at all and nor does it require the purchaser to borrow the total amount of the purchase price and then repay it. The purchaser simply signs the contract, moves in to the property and commences payments of rent and equity purchase instalments, which are combined in a single payment called a residency fee.

The amount of this increases every year but the schedule of payments is set for five years at a time so that purchasers can budget with confidence. There is a single initial fee of £600 payable at the time of signing the contract but this is the only initial outlay. There is no stamp duty liability until completion of the purchase of the full amount of equity. This is scheduled to take twenty-five years but the period can be extended. In the case of a customer experiencing financial problems, there is flexibility to freeze equity purchase payments and take rental payments out of the acquired equity, or to sell equity back to Gentoo, which makes it less likely that the occupiers will lose their home in the event of a reduction in income. Although purchasers do not legally own the property until all payments have been completed, Gentoo maintains that they have the same rights and responsibilities as home owners from the outset and that these are set out in a 'security arrangement', which compares favourably with the ambiguity that surrounds the status of the purchaser as owner or tenant in the documentation of some Islamic providers of home finance.[18]

This radically innovative scheme was introduced in October 2011 on a small number of newly built housing developments in several towns in the north-east of England. It received substantial coverage in the regional press and attracted many times more enquiries than there were homes available under the scheme. The Gentoo executive in charge of the scheme admitted that he was himself surprised by the extent of interest.[19] So it is evident that such a scheme is badly needed, and it is sad that its Islamic basis remains unknown to the general public. The Genie scheme is described in the information material as a Home Purchase Plan, the same term used for Islamic home finance arrangements. Natalie Elphicke has confirmed that 'my own inspiration [was] from the ethical basis of the Islamic residential financing approach which was very much in tune with the client's social commitment and aspirations for the Genie product'.[20]

There are several obvious limitations on the scheme. It is not a substitute for social rented housing, as applicants need to be credit checked in the same way as for a conventional mortgage and have an annual household income of at least £18,000, which is low by national standards but still higher than some households in deprived areas can achieve. It is only available for the purchase of Gentoo's own properties, at the present time mostly newly built ones, because it is structured around buying a home directly from the builder. It would be difficult to operate on a large-scale commercial basis, although if housing developers continue to find themselves with large numbers of unsold properties on their hands because of the reduction in mortgage lending, such a solution could look more attractive. Furthermore it is not clear to what extent Gentoo has intellectual property in the scheme which would limit its adoption by other companies. This information is at present being protected as commercially sensitive. The most likely interpretation would seem to be that Gentoo has the rights to a particular contractual form branded as Genie, but the fundamental principle of offering house purchase on an increasing ownership basis is free to be adapted by other suppliers.

The implications of secular ethical home finance for Islamic home finance

Building societies' use of conventional interest naturally makes them unacceptable to the most devout Muslims, but they appear ethically preferable to conventional banks to some Muslim as well as non-Muslim observers, and some writers on Islamic finance have begun to explore the possibilities of adapting the mutual structure to an Islamic financial context. Usman Hayat is one such. He comments that '[h]istorically a mutual legal structure has been common in ethical finance' but that '[m]utuality has not been the structure of choice in Islamic finance'. Although he has concerns about the practicalities of raising sufficient capital under a mutual structure he feels that its wider adoption in Islamic finance could 'help allay the fears of those who see modern Islamic finance as Shari'ah arbitrage, where, in the name of religion, Muslims are asked to pay more to for-profit companies for what is otherwise available for less'.[21] It seems likely that a younger generation of British Muslim scholars will explore the British tradition of mutualism and seek to extend its use in Islamic products beyond *takaful*.

In secular home finance which markets itself as ethical, inclusivity and accessibility are key components of the ethical aspirations of the brand. The mutual society tradition outlined in this chapter is primarily concerned to help ordinary people buy their own homes and to promote other social goals regarded as desirable. The Islamic home finance sector by contrast is primarily concerned with formal observance of religious prescriptions. This is presumably because *Shari'ah* compliant finance in the UK is at present provided only by a small number of large commercial banks whose Islamic divisions have no wider social goals beyond attracting more British Muslims as customers. There are signs that younger British Muslims are becoming dissatisfied with this situation and increasingly demanding that Islamic providers who routinely position their products as part of the wider ethical sector should make more attempt to adopt some of the other concerns of the sector.[22] In the field of home finance that means addressing the situation of lower-income Muslims who are at present excluded from property ownership.

Furthermore, one of the most important characteristics of Islamic financial structures generally is the emphasis on their being based on real assets. While this does not necessarily mean property, and Islamic banks in other countries make greater use of other forms of business assets, Islamic providers in the UK have relied heavily on property as the underlying asset, both commercial and residential. This is due to a number of factors, but the cultural importance of property ownership in Britain and the housing experiences of migrant Muslims in the country have both played an important role. This has recently led to concerns about the scale of the sector's exposure to falling property values. An aspect less often discussed is whether the emphasis on property as an investment conflicts with the socially desirable aim of providing affordable housing to every family. Can the reliance on rising property prices and rent levels, which will exclude increasing numbers from the housing market, be seen as in some sense un-ethical?

Notes

1. I am indebted to the interesting exhibition on the history of the companies now comprising the Halifax Bank of Scotland Group which is located within the group's headquarters on the Mound, Edinburgh.
2. HM Treasury, *The Future of Building Societies*, July 2012, p. 7. All of the figures in this paragraph are taken from this document. It is available to download from www.hm-treasury.gov.uk and from the websites of some building societies.
3. This information is found in both *The Future of Building Societies*, p. 9 and in the factsheet *What is a Building Society?* produced by the Building Societies Association and available on www.bsa.org.uk.
4. HM Treasury, *Banking Reform: Delivering Stability and Supporting a Sustainable Economy*, June 2012, p. 30. This White

Paper sets out the government's proposals for implementing the recommendations of the Independent Commission on Banking, and is available for download from www.hm-treasury. gov.uk.

5. www.bsa.org.uk (accessed on 31 July 2012).

6. Press release by the Building Societies Association on 30 August 2012, available from www.bsa.org.uk.

7. *The Future of Building Societies*, p. 9.

8. A useful list of demutualised societies and their subsequent fates is provided on www.bsa.org.uk. The Building Societies Association is anxious to ensure that these renegade former members are never mistakenly referred to as if they were still mutuals.

9. A convenient summary of the events leading up to the near collapse of Northern Rock, the highest-profile former mutual, can be found in Cable, Vince (2009), *The Storm*, London: Atlantic, pp. 9–14.

10. www.bsa.org.uk.

11. www.ecology.co.uk (accessed on 3 September 2012).

12. www.bsa.org.uk/docs/consumerpdfs/assets.

13. All these figures are taken from a press release dated 26 March 2012, available on www.ecology.co.uk.

14. Press release dated 29 June 2012, available on www.ecology. co.uk.

15. Personal communication from Anna Laycock, of the Ecology, dated 31 July 2012.

16. www.bsa.org.uk.

17. All these figures are taken from the report on 2011 sent to members prior to the April 2012 AGM.

18. These details of the scheme are taken from www.justaskgenie. co.uk (accessed on 3 September 2012).

19. 'Gentoo acquires new homes to satisfy demand for Genie', *Newcastle Journal*, 25 November 2012.

20. Personal communication dated 12 December 2011.

21. Hayat, Usman, 'Islamic or ethical finance: where is its future in European retail markets?', *New Horizon* magazine, October 2010.
22. Personal conversation with Arwa Aburawa on 9 January 2012.

CHAPTER 5

DEBT AND CREDIT

The central tenet of Islamic finance is of course the prohibition of the payment or receipt of bank interest. Some writing on the subject discusses this principle in a somewhat abstract way. This chapter seeks to take a wider view of the debt and credit landscape in modern Britain. It discusses the work of some non-Muslim groups which, while not opposed in principle to all interest, believe that some forms of interest-based credit are more unethical than others, and argues that a concentration on the details of *Shari'ah* compliant models should not cause those working in Islamic finance to lose sight of these distinctions.

Indebtedness from an ethical perspective

Traditionally, immigrant Muslim families in Britain with religiously based objections to borrowing at interest would simply do without anything which could not be bought outright. There were also some cultural differences in spending priorities, which has generated an academic debate on whether some commonly used measures of deprivation may be inappropriate for minority communities. Should a family who lack some commonly found household items but who have no debt be considered poorer than one which has all of them but at the cost of a large outstanding credit card balance? Possibly the greatest challenge to the Islamic finance industry at present is finding a way to produce an entirely *Shari'ah* compliant credit card. To date none of the mechanisms used have met with general scholarly approval.[1] This may not be a bad thing, as the lack of any form of *Shari'ah* compliant lending in Britain until recently has arguably protected British Muslims from incurring the high levels of indebtedness which became increasingly common and acceptable among the general population over the fifty years or so since Muslims first arrived in the country. The increasing integration of second-generation Muslims into mainstream purchasing and banking practices seems likely to increase their levels of indebtedness.

The Conservative governments of the 1980s introduced a deregulation of financial services which led to an enormous increase in the number of credit products offered by banks and other providers. In addition to increasing the availability of home purchase loans, it also encouraged home ownership by other legislative means. This led to a substantial and permanent change in the pattern of housing tenure in Britain, with a large fall in the percentage of people occupying social housing and a large increase in the proportion owning their own home, or at least working hard to repay a mortgage for its purchase. This in turn caused many of the generation who were young adults in the 1980s to look to the increase in the value of their houses as their main route to prosperity and financial security in their old age. Their children were brought up to expect to do the same, but now in many cases find themselves excluded from home ownership by the sharp reduction in bank lending. Both generations came to take for granted the easy availability of credit cards and personal bank loans and in many cases believed that these technically 'unsecured' debts were in some sense underwritten by the steady increase in the value of their real estate.

It has been argued powerfully by some left-leaning writers[2] that the explosion in the availability of credit over this period disguised the increase in social and economic inequality which also came about over the last few decades, by enabling people to engage in conspicuous consumption which was not based on their actual means. The reliance on increasing property prices has been summed up with brutal frankness as a process whereby 'more and more people became heavily indebted in the hope of acquiring freedom from debt'.[3] This is something which should be borne in mind in discussions of Islamic home purchase finance or any other form of lending which presents itself as 'ethical'. There are ethical issues involved in property purchase more fundamental than simply the technical details of the finance involved.

The present situation

Credit Action describes itself as 'a money advice charity', and it monitors trends in indebtedness in the UK.[4] The most recent figures show that unsecured debt (which in essence means everything except home purchase loans) has been on a downward trend for some time. This is likely to be due mostly to the greater difficulty of obtaining credit since the banking crisis rather than to any dramatic change of attitude to it. The charity points out that the fall in credit card debt may not be an unqualified good as part of the reason for it is that customers who can no longer obtain credit from banks have been driven to seek it from other providers who charge much higher rates of interest.

In June 2012 the amount of outstanding unsecured debt in the UK was around £207 billion, or an average figure per household of £7,854 (the average annual salary is around £26,000 before tax). Outstanding debt on home purchase mortgages was £1.24 trillion, or an average per household of just under £50,000, which is rather less than one-third of the average house price. Averaging the figure in this way is however misleading as it obscures very great differences in the distribution of debt. Credit Action estimates that 105 properties are repossessed by the mortgage lender every day at the time of writing. The charity also offers the startling statistic that around £14 million of debt of all kinds is written off by lenders every day in the UK. While banks which have been obliged to write off loans are not generally regarded as deserving of much sympathy from the general public, the long-term effects on the stability of the banking system and of the economy generally of losses on this scale are worrying.

While the total amount of debt owed may have fallen somewhat, the rise in unemployment over the last few years has meant that the numbers of people struggling to keep up repayments on their credit agreements has increased. This increase in unmanageable debts has produced a corresponding proliferation of agencies trying to help. As a rule the financial services industry is supportive of debt advice agencies (sometimes even financially supportive) as lenders realise that they are more likely to recover at least some of their money from borrowers who are receiving advice to manage repayments sensibly than from those who are left to cope unaided with a downward spiral of growing arrears made worse by the addition of interest and punitive charges.

The national network of Citizens Advice Bureaux (CAB) is the first port of call for many people with problems of all kinds. CAB debt specialists can work out a budget and repayment plan and negotiate with creditors by letter and phone on behalf of clients. They do not however offer a complete debt management service in the sense of making the repayments on the client's behalf. Many debt clients would like to surrender all their paperwork to the bureau but it is CAB policy to refuse, as it is believed to be important that clients take responsibility for repayments themselves.[5]

National Debtline is a service offered by the Money Advice Trust, another charity, in this case one set up specifically to help with debt problems. It offers advice on a free phone number which is staffed for long hours every weekday and also by email. There are, in addition, some local debt advice agencies operating only in particular areas of the country, funded by a mixture of public money and charitable donations.

So there is no shortage of free, impartial advice available to anyone with debt problems. Despite this, there is a persistent problem with companies operating on the margins of legality by offering to manage clients' debts in return for large fees which in the long run will only worsen their situation.[6] Some companies have crossed over into the realm of fraud and pursue debt-ridden members of the public with unfounded claims to know some way of having their debts written off, naturally in exchange for a large advance fee. It is evident that such attempts to exploit for one's own financial gain people who are in a difficult and vulnerable situation are unethical by any definition. However, organisations motivated by religious conviction rather than greed present a more complex challenge to our understanding of what ethical behaviour in the world of financial services means.

Christians Against Poverty

Christians Against Poverty (CAP) is an interesting example of an organisation working in the field of money advice with an explicitly Christian ethos and motivation. It was founded in 1996 by John Kirkby, who had worked in the financial services industry for seventeen years but had also had a period of unemployment and hardship. After undergoing a Christian conversion experience he felt 'called' to use his professional expertise to help the poor. His original vision was to start a Christian bank or building society[7] but he was obliged to abandon that idea because of the huge amount of start-up capital needed. It is not clear whether he was aware at that time of the existence of Kingdom Bank. (This Christian bank is discussed in Chapter 2, 'Retail Banking'.) He eventually decided that debt counselling was the most useful field to enter. Christians Against Poverty has now expanded to a network of 205 centres throughout the UK, all based in churches, with a target of 500. It has also spread overseas, to Australia, New Zealand and Canada. It appears to be run in a thoroughly professional way and to be well regarded within the financial services industry. It has received a number of industry awards, most prominently Debt Counsellor of the Year in the 2011 round of the awards sponsored by *Credit Today* magazine.

John Kirkby's home town is Bradford in West Yorkshire. He first set up CAP in Bradford and the organisation's head office is still located there, in a building which was formerly one of the many derelict mills left behind after the collapse of the textile industry in the area. The building is now called Jubilee Mill, an invocation of the references in the Hebrew scriptures to 'years of jubilee' when debtors were freed from their obligations. The fact that Bradford has a large Muslim population and is popularly regarded as a centre of Islamic rather than Christian activism raises some interesting points. The work of CAP provides a valuable reminder that poverty is not confined to any one ethnic or religious group and that the common experience of living in a deprived area makes people of all backgrounds perceive this kind of work to be necessary. CAP's advertising material states that its services are available to people of any faith or no faith, and the size of the Muslim population locally invites the question of whether it has any Muslim clients. Until recently the answer to this seemed to be in the negative, but a Muslim woman has now appeared among the clients whose stories are featured on CAP's website.[8] She states that she was 'apprehensive' about approaching CAP because she is Muslim, but felt 'so comfortable' with the adviser and now recommends the service highly. This suggests that there may be a need for a similar service tailored to clients of Muslim background.

The evangelical Christian agenda of CAP is quite overt. Its website appeals to churches for support in these terms:

> We believe that the church is the hope of the world. It holds in its hands the only message that can change lives and communities both now and for eternity. That's why our services are always run in partnership with a local church ... Your church can partner with Christians Against Poverty to bring hope and salvation to those living in debt and poverty on your doorstep, through our first class debt counselling service.[9]

John Kirkby's autobiography, *Nevertheless*, a copy of which is sent free to anyone who requests one, makes it clear that his vision was always to bring people to 'know the Lord' and not just to free them from debt. In Jubilee Mill a bell is rung every time a case worker reports that a client has been 'saved', that is, has decided to embrace Christianity. The type of language employed by Mr Kirkby and by the organisation as a whole blurs the distinction between being freed from the burden of debt in a purely literal sense and being freed from the burden of sin in a Biblical sense. The quotation above provides one illustration of this in the use of the word 'salvation' with a double meaning.

The link between the concepts of sin and of debt in Judeo-Christian tradition is ancient and the two words are closely related etymologically. For example, in modern German the word *Schuld* still means both guilt and monetary debt. Weber quotes John Bunyan, writing in the seventeenth century, explaining that we may through virtue be able to pay off the interest but never by any means the principal of the debt to God created by our sin.[10] Weber describes this as a 'tasteless' image, but it may be more accurate to say that it brings out a concept implicit in Christianity with unusual frankness. The core belief of Christianity is that Jesus 'died for our sins', that his voluntary surrender to death represented a kind of payment or compensation for the sins of all humanity, and that therefore God does not require individuals to pay for their own sins as they did before the coming of Jesus Christ. The detailed theology behind this belief is somewhat hard to follow for the ordinary believer, but at a rhetorical level it is central to Christians' understanding of their faith, and modern evangelicals tend to emphasise the promise of being freed from the debt owed by sin if one will only accept Christ into one's life. With this in mind, a less committed reader of John Kirkby's account of his decision to found a debt counselling service may wonder if it was the centrality of this imagery in his faith which prompted him to choose this particular form of financial service rather than any of the others he could usefully have chosen.

The strength of CAP's motivation to change lives leads it to adopt an approach to clients which is more prescriptive than that normally favoured by secular debt advice services. Clients are required to hand over all the paperwork related to their financial affairs, to leave CAP to negotiate directly with their creditors, and to make a regular payment into a

CAP account which will then be used to repay their debts, to pay their utility bills and even to build up savings. This contrasts with the approach taken by, for example, the Citizens Advice Bureaux, described above. It appears that CAP clients are encouraged to identify the sense of overwhelming relief often felt after handing over all responsibility for dealing with creditors as an experience of the love of God.

In addition to helping with debts, CAP also offers a course in money management. This has been very successful and now has tailored versions for students, schoolchildren and prisoners. There is also a specialist service for church leaders and ministers. There is a dedicated confidential helpline for such clients, who are also permitted to take the money management course at home, whereas all other clients are required to attend a group. CAP explains that this is to deal with the particular difficulties of experiencing financial problems whilst being in a leadership position and expected to provide a role model. It seems also to involve a certain protection of the image of church leaders.

The extraordinary paradox of John Kirkby's story is that his overwhelming faith in his mission drove him to behave with an improvidence much more extreme than that of most of his clients. He gave up well-paid employment and made himself ineligible for welfare benefits by stating firmly that he was not prepared to accept another job. He told his creditors when they telephoned that he could not pay them because he was now working full-time in Christian ministry and interpreted their chilly response to this news as a sign of the lack of religious faith in the financial services industry. Soon after he founded CAP he and his wife were £4,000 in arrears with their mortgage payments and the lender had begun repossession proceedings. Even their fellow Christians, on whose generosity the Kirkbys were forced to rely, told him he was expanding CAP too fast and too recklessly. His lack of any sense of irony about his behaviour is sometimes faintly comic. On one occasion he wrote in his diary that he would be forced to use his credit card to purchase basic essentials and did not feel comfortable about this, but thought that perhaps God was calling him to use the Visa card as a test of his faith that the money would appear to repay it.[11] One imagines that a CAP client who produced the same justification for outstanding credit card debts would be unlikely to receive a sympathetic hearing.

CAP was originally funded by grants from various trusts and funds, some Christian and some concerned with poverty relief generally, and by donations from churches and individual supporters. It now has a well established base of supporters who pay regular contributions, whom it calls Life Changers. In 2011 these regular commitments accounted for 38 per cent of its income. Most of the rest of its income is derived from churches and from single donations from individuals, including clients, who sometimes make donations out of the savings element of their CAP accounts. An impressive 8 per cent of the organisation's income comes from the financial services industry itself under a scheme whereby creditors who have received regular repayments through CAP agree to donate 10 per cent of their value to the organisation to help other clients.[12] Receiving funding from private sources rather than public bodies has in the long term been an advantage to CAP by giving it more freedom of action. For example, when case workers first meet clients who are facing serious hardship they sometimes buy food for them, which debt services answerable to the taxpayer would not be permitted to do.

In 1999 CAP applied for and received funding of £225,000 over three years from the body which awards grants from the funds raised by the National Lottery. Because many Christians are strongly opposed to gambling, the decision to apply for lottery money caused a great deal of argument and soul-searching within the organisation. It eventually resolved the dilemma by taking the view that if God disapproved of this source of funding he would ensure that the application was refused. CAP was also careful to make clear on the submission that one of the objectives of the charity was 'the advancement of the Christian faith'.[13]

From the outset John Kirkby took the view that CAP would not make use of volunteers but would pay all its workers a decent salary. He cites the Biblical text 'the labourer is worthy of his reward' (1 Timothy 5: 18) in justification of this. CAP now offers an internship programme which pays the participants bursaries, in contrast to the unpaid internships which are increasingly prevalent. This is an admirable principle which other organisations would do well to emulate. There is a point where voluntary work motivated by a desire to help the community becomes exploitation, and there are well documented concerns over the tendency of unpaid internships to give privileged access to employment to those from more affluent backgrounds.

Unfortunately, in the early days of CAP the impact of this principle was considerably lessened in practice by the fact that the organisation kept on recruiting staff without any guarantee that it would be able to pay them, and frequently did not pay them in full (the account given in *Nevertheless* makes this clear throughout). The staff were often asked to divide up whatever money was available for salaries according to who needed it the most, and were under pressure to minimise their statements of how much they needed. CAP only recruited committed Christians who believed, or at least said they did, that God would provide eventually if they only trusted him. The ethos of the organisation also dictated the purchase of only the best-quality office equipment, regardless of cost. At the worst periods CAP was unable to pay its office suppliers. The phrase repeatedly used by John Kirkby to describe this process of routinely living beyond his and the organisation's means is 'stepping out in faith'. He was critical of the lack of faith of a CAP trustee who 'argued very strongly [for] reducing our expenditure to our expected income'.[14] There is an element of the so-called 'prosperity gospel' about this – that is, the belief that the acquisition of wealth is a sign of God's favour. It might appear to an impartial observer that Mr Kirkby was just blessed with exceptionally generous and forbearing friends, but in his eyes every act of assistance was money sent by God as a sign that his work was divinely approved and blessed.

The story of Christians Against Poverty raises issues about the relationship between religiously motivated financial activism and what is generally understood by ethical corporate behaviour. For a start, knowingly embarking on a development programme which will leave an organisation unable to pay its staff, its suppliers or its tax liabilities would not satisfy the most basic ethical criteria anywhere outside an atmosphere of intense religious faith. More fundamentally, there is a real question about whether tying help with debts so closely to evangelism is unethical by the standards of the wider world, since it appears to involve a risk of being emotionally manipulative of vulnerable people. This danger is recognised in the Charity Commission's guidelines on religious proselytism by charities, which indicate that 'exerting improper pressure on people in distress or need' would breach the requirements that 'the advancement of religion' must not involve 'detriment or harm' to the public.[15]

John Kirkby's account of the purchase of Jubilee Mill describes a finance model intriguingly close to an Islamic *sukuk*. He persuaded some trusts and wealthy individuals to give money for the purchase and restoration of the building with the promise that it would be an investment rather than an outright gift because CAP would pay them a return on their contribution, which would be 'like rent' for it, structured as the payment of a proportion of the equity in the building to donors.[16] He was not of course aware of any similarities to the Islamic tradition, believing it to be an innovation inspired by the Christian commitment of his supporters. This demonstrates that any financial model which supplies a real need is likely to be developed independently more than once.

Credit unions

Credit unions are a well-established institution in British life and have enjoyed consistent support from governments of all political persuasions. Politicians of the left like them because they help the poorest members of society; those of the right approve because they promote self-help and thrift. Their umbrella organisation is the Association of British Credit Unions Limited (ABCUL). Any credit union which subscribes to ABCUL's code of practice can become a member. At the time of writing there are about 400 credit unions in the UK with about a million members. They hold savings of £762 million and have about £604 million out on loan.[17]

The origins of credit unions lie in the same nineteenth-century tradition of mutualism which produced building societies, but they had no recognised legal structure or governance until as recently as 1979 when the Labour government of the day passed the Credit Unions Act. Under this Act it is a requirement that the members of a union have 'a common bond' of some kind; they are not permitted to accept all-comers. The most usual basis for membership is living in a certain defined geographical area. There are also unions open only to those who work for a particular employer or belong to a particular trade union or church. They are all co-operatives and distribute all their profits to members in the form of an annual dividend, with no external shareholders. Directors are elected from among the membership by the members. The core function of a credit union is to facilitate small-scale savings and loans, but recently some of them have introduced current accounts. Many offer life insurance free to all members, with loans paid off on the death of a member and a bonus on top of the accumulated savings paid to a member's heirs.

The maximum rate of interest which a credit union can charge on a loan is 2 per cent per month on the reducing balance, which equates to an APR of 26.8 per cent. This is not particularly low when compared to the APR of a typical credit card. However this is a maximum and many credit unions charge less than this. The one with which the writer is most familiar, Northumberland Credit Union (NCUL), charges 1 per cent per month and regards this rate as competitive with bank loans for sums of up to £2,000.[18] Direct comparison with credit cards and bank loans is not entirely fair as credit union loans are typically for small amounts over short periods, often smaller and shorter than a bank would be prepared to consider. What is more, many members of credit unions are excluded from bank credit products because they are unemployed or for other reasons on very low incomes, so the alternatives open to them in practice are those lenders charging extortionate interest rates considered below.

All credit unions encourage members to save as well as to borrow, and insist that all members save for a certain period before being eligible to borrow. This is how it works in practice, again using Northumberland Credit Union as an example: all members pay an initial joining fee of £2 and must then save at least £4 weekly for a minimum of eight weeks before being eligible for any loan. They may then borrow up to £100 more than they have saved. For example, a member who has saved £10 per week for eight weeks would be eligible to borrow £180. If the first loan is repaid in full within thirty-nine weeks, the member becomes eligible for a loan of up to twice the amount saved. If that is repaid, the member may then borrow up to three times the amount saved, with the maximum loan being four times savings, up to a ceiling of £3,000. All members are encouraged to continue making their regular savings payment at the same time as repaying their loans. Although credit unions are aimed especially at people who cannot access banking services and make most payments by cash, NCUL also accepts payments by standing order. This union does not pay any interest on savings held by adults, but it does pay 3 per cent a year on 'junior' accounts, to encourage children to get into the habit of saving.

This appears to be a shining example of responsible lending, 'know your customer' prudence and encouragement of thrift. It is difficult to find anything to criticise about credit unions, and indeed almost nobody ever does criticise them. So the puzzling aspect is why they are not more widely used. A membership of one million, whilst it represents, according to ABCUL, a figure which has nearly doubled in the last fifteen years or so, is still a tiny proportion of the number of people in Britain who could benefit from membership of a credit union. Why is anybody still falling into the clutches of high interest lenders?

Most obviously, the requirement to save before borrowing deters many of the poorest and those with the most unpredictable lives. Then there are problems in organising unions on the scale needed to reach those most in need of them. They are mostly reliant on volunteers to run them and this means that their provision varies considerably in different areas of the country and their accessibility can be erratic even within the same area. It is hard to find premises in which to hold paying-in sessions and those that are available cheaply may be run-down and off-putting to potential clients. Funding is a constant challenge, because even on the small scale on which they operate, they require start-up capital which may be difficult to obtain. Credit unions also suffer from an image problem, in that they are perceived to cater only for the very poorest people and those who have no bank accounts. This results in a certain stigma being attached to them in the minds of those who do have access to conventional banking.

There are now though signs that this may be changing and credit unions are beginning to attract the attention of those looking for alternative financial solutions out of conviction and not just necessity. *Ethical Consumer* magazine and website has published articles strongly supportive of credit unions, calling on readers to use their savings to support local mutual organisations rather than the big banks.[19] The popular website *Moneysaving Expert* with its TV presenter host Martin Lewis has stated that credit unions are 'sadly under-publicised' and that they sometimes 'offer products that beat mainstream finance'.[20] ABCUL itself now makes a point of describing the services credit unions offer as 'ethical', which one guesses may not have been the primary concern of the earliest members.

The present government has stated that it would like credit unions to expand, and in January 2012 the regulations which govern them were amended in order to promote this. The 'common bond' criterion of membership has been relaxed to enable unions to serve more than one qualifying group of people. They will also be free to set their own rules on whether members should be allowed to maintain their membership after losing their original eligibility through changing job or moving house. There are still restrictions on the 'field' of potential members, to ensure that a good service can be offered to all of them. Unions may now accept associations and corporate entities as members and not just individuals, although non-individual members are limited to 10 per cent of the total. The thinking behind this is that they will be better able to serve community groups by enrolling them as a whole and better able to access funds by enabling groups who support their aims to deposit funds with them. Religious groups are specifically mentioned as an example in ABCUL's briefing note. The most significant change is that which allows unions to pay a fixed rate of interest on savings rather than a share of the profits as a dividend. The hope here is that permitting a direct comparison of the rate of return offered by credit unions with that paid by banks will make it easier to publicise competitive savings products and thus attract more deposits.[21] The next step envisaged by ABCUL is to establish a partnership with the Post Office which would result in an enormous increase in the ease of accessing credit union services. (The role of the Post Office in promoting more inclusive financial services is discussed in Chapter 2, 'Retail Banking'.)

Considered from an Islamic point of view, this shift to fixed interest is of course a step in the wrong direction and may lessen the attractiveness of credit unions to practising Muslims. In their fundamental principles however – those of mutual aid offered to members with all profits retained and no money transferred outside the qualifying group – credit unions have a close similarity both to *takaful* models and to the *kameti* savings groups common among the first generation of Muslim immigrants to the UK. Within the regulations which govern them they have considerable flexibility to do whatever best suits their members, and they are not obliged to pay interest instead of dividends, or even to charge interest, if they can manage to fund themselves without doing so. Whether formal credit unions affiliated to the national body can develop out of the traditional informal mutual aid arrangements among Muslim communities remains to be seen.

Extreme *riba* in the present day

So-called 'payday lenders' have received a considerable amount of media attention recently. These are companies which advance fairly small sums for a period initially of no more than a month to people who can provide proof of employment, in the expectation of being repaid when the customer receives their monthly salary. Such companies are found in most town centres now but they specialise in operating online, where their ease of access and the speed with which the loan funds are transferred to the customer's bank account makes them particularly attractive to those who either need the money urgently or are accustomed to doing most things online and find conventional banks slow or intimidating. They typically charge very high rates of interest. For example, someone who borrows £400 for thirty days from Wonga will have to repay £525.48.[22] Borrowers often find that because of this there is an even bigger gap between their income and their expenditure next month and therefore have to borrow more and more until their debt becomes unmanageable. At present there is no regulation of the interest rates which such lenders can charge, but regulatory bodies are closely monitoring their activities.

The recent phenomenon of 'payday' lending has had greater publicity than more traditional forms of high interest lending, particularly the kind known colloquially as 'doorstep' lending, or more formally as home credit. This may be because the latter operates in a world which escapes the notice of many financial journalists. It is used mostly by people who do not have a payday – the unemployed and people who cannot work because of health problems or childcare responsibilities.

The inappropriately named Provident is a leader in the home credit market. Its APR is 272 per cent, a bargain compared with some of the payday lenders, but extortionate by the standards of people who deal with banks. The maximum amount it will lend initially is the remarkably low figure of £500, which is a fairly clear indicator of the type of customer it targets. Customer statements in its advertising material confirm that these loans are taken out most commonly to cover bills for basic necessities such as fuel and to buy presents for the family at Christmas. (Somehow Christmas, one of the major Christian festivals, has become the most predictable cause of hardship and debt. All debt counselling agencies report their highest level of enquiries in January. It is to be hoped that the custom of exchanging gifts at Eid al-Fitr does not result in the same phenomenon.)

Although Provident does have a website, customers always have to meet an agent face to face in order to take out a loan, and all of the transactions are carried out in cash and in person. They say that 'all our agents are friendly, helpful local people'.[23] The testimonials from clients all mention how friendly the agents are, 'like one of the family', 'always does her best for us'. Existing customers are paid £10 for referring a friend who takes out a loan. Clients reportedly prioritise repayment of this type of loan over more urgent needs because of having a personal relationship with the collector.[24] This is a manipulation of friendship networks to form a marketing tool. It is as it were the dark side of mutual aid. Nevertheless it should be borne in mind that home credit lenders are offering a service to very high-risk borrowers who are often in desperate need of money, and that well-intentioned legislation which makes this commercially unviable by reducing the interest rates which can be charged is very likely to leave such borrowers with no option but illegal money-lenders.

The Office of Fair Trading (OFT) has produced a statement of guidance on irresponsible lending. The most recent version was produced after a consultation to which a very wide range of interested parties responded, including the Institute of Islamic Banking and Insurance.[25] It forms a convenient summary of bad practice in credit provision. The peculiar interest for readers of this book is the similarity between the modern censure of the OFT and the Quranic passages which form the foundation of the Islamic prohibition of *riba*. The OFT particularly criticises 'repeatedly refinancing (or "rolling-over")' loans, 'where the overall effect is to increase the borrower's indebtedness in an unsustainable manner', and arrangements whereby 'the borrower can elect to "renew" the loan for a fee and delay payment for a further agreed period of time'.[26] The Quran warns: 'devour not usury, doubling and quadrupling' (3: 130) which commentators consider to be a reference to precisely this practice of extending the period of the loan for a debtor who cannot pay on time at the cost of a very large increase in the amount owed.

Of course the OFT guidelines do not impinge on those lenders who operate outside the law altogether. It is a legal requirement to have a credit licence in order to lend money. Those lenders who operate without a licence are popularly referred to as 'loan sharks'. There is a government project which is attempting to close down their activities by encouraging people to report them[27]. Illegal lenders are still using the sort of tactics which angered Prophet Muhammad fourteen centuries ago. Violence, sexual coercion and seizure of welfare benefits paperwork are reportedly used to force repayment, while arbitrary amounts are often added to the sum owed so that no matter how many payments are made it never reduces.

The implications of the wider credit and debt situation for Islamic financial services

The main point here is that nothing essential has changed since the days of the Prophet, or since the time Jesus railed against corrupt money-changers and tax collectors. Human nature never really alters, and neither does the way the rich will tend to abuse their power over the poor. We should not become so absorbed in the finer points of *Shari'ah* compliance in products aimed at those who have no problem obtaining credit on attractive terms that we lose sight of the fact that *riba* in its most blatant form is still very much in existence and is the only option for many of the less privileged.

Those people most vulnerable to high interest lenders are hard to reach by government or by charities working in financial education. They often cannot afford to have internet access at home and sometimes have poor standards of literacy which makes them reluctant to engage with any form of printed information. This is an area where religious groups are in a good position to help those who are hard for other agencies to reach. The close ties and high levels of trust among worshipping congregations and other faith groups form a good basis for offering help in a tactful way to members who seem to be struggling.

It seems likely that indebtedness among Muslims is under-reported because of the sensitivity of the topic of borrowing at interest, and that there is a need for culturally appropriate advice services. The secular debt counselling agencies offer an excellent service and follow a rigorously confidential, non-directive and non-judgemental approach, but may not appreciate the particular problems and needs of those of Muslim heritage. Christian work in this area is valuable but Muslims are likely to feel uncomfortable about the encroachment of explicitly Christian services into Muslim communities. The challenge is to develop debt counselling which combines the high standards of the secular services with an Islamic cultural sensitivity. Funding such an agency would be an excellent 'corporate social responsibility' project for an Islamic bank, and would do much to extend the reach of Islamic finance into disadvantaged Muslim communities.

Notes

1. These are discussed in Housby, Elaine (2011), *Islamic Financial Services in the United Kingdom*, Edinburgh: Edinburgh University Press, pp. 69–74.
2. See Cruddas, John and Rutherford, Jonathan, (2010), 'The common table', in Williams, Rowan and Elliott, Larry (eds) *Crisis and Recovery: Ethics, Economics and Justice*, London: Palgrave, pp. 56–7.
3. Blond, Phillip (2010), 'There is no wealth but life', in Williams, Rowan and Elliott, Larry (eds) *Crisis and Recovery: Ethics, Economics and Justice*, London: Palgrave, p. 83.
4. All of the figures in these two paragraphs are taken from www.creditaction.org.uk (accessed on 21 August 2012).
5. Personal conversations with Citizens Advice Bureau staff, particularly Gillian Arnold.
6. All of the debt advice agencies discussed in this section mention this problem in their information material.
7. Kirkby, John (2011), *Nevertheless*, Bradford: CAP Books, pp. 30–1.
8. *Zahraa's Story* on www.capuk.org (accessed on 14 August 2012).

9. www.capuk.org (accessed on 14 August 2012).

10. Weber, Max ([1930] 2001), *The Protestant Ethic and the Spirit of Capitalism*, London: Routledge, p. 77.

11. Kirkby, *Nevertheless*, p. 93.

12. All these figures are taken from *CAP Client Report 2011*, Appendix 1. Available to download from www.capuk.org.

13. Kirkby, *Nevertheless*, p. 108.

14. Kirkby *Nevertheless*, p. 113.

15. 'The advancement of religion for the public benefit', amended December 2011, Annex B, a publication by the Charity Commission, available on www.charity-commission.gov.uk. The regulations on religious charities are considered in detail in Chapter 7, 'Charities'.

16. Kirkby, *Nevertheless*, pp. 131–3.

17. All of the information in these three paragraphs is taken from www.abcul.coop (accessed on 20 August 2012).

18. All of the information about Northumberland Credit Union is taken from www.ncul.co.uk (accessed on 13 December 2012).

19. www.ethicalconsumer.org (accessed on 20 August 2012).

20. www.moneysavingexpert.com (accessed on 20 August 2012).

21. All these details are taken from the ABCUL, *Briefing on Legislative Change*, available on www.abcul.coop.

22. www.wonga.com (accessed on 24 August 2012).

23. www.providentpersonalcredit.com (accessed on 24 August 2012).

24. Personal conversations with Citizens Advice Bureau staff, particularly Gillian Arnold.

25. *Summary of Responses to the Consultation on 'Irresponsible Lending – OFT Guidance for Creditors'*, August 2010, p. 89. Available to download from www.oft.gov.uk.

26. *Irresponsible Lending – OFT Guidance for Creditors*, March

2010, updated February 2011, p. 63. Available to download from www.oft.gov.uk.

27. www.direct.gov.uk/stoploansharks (accessed on 24 August 2012).

CHAPTER 6
SOCIAL
ENTERPRISE

The term 'social enterprise' has appeared in recent years to describe forms of business activity which have as their main aim some social good rather than the making of profit for its own sake. In some quarters such social business is regarded as preferable to traditional charity as a way of raising funds for worthwhile causes. The phenomenon is of particular interest in relation to Islamic finance because the Islamic tradition offers well developed models of entrepreneurship and venture capital, which could easily be adapted to social rather than profit-oriented ends. This chapter begins with an overview of the social enterprise sector in Britain at the present time, considers how the Islamic tradition fits in with this, and then gives some detailed case studies of examples which present particular points of interest in this context.

The political climate

The general political climate of the UK at the present time is very favourable to social enterprise. Things were already moving in this direction under the previous Labour government, which developed the concept of the 'third way' in politics between socialism and the unfettered free market and sought to encourage the voluntary sector to play more of a role in the delivery of public services. The present government, a coalition between the Conservative and Liberal Democrat parties, has continued this increased emphasis on the role of the voluntary sector and has also promoted the idea that entrepreneurship can be a means of delivering social change more effectively than through state action. This enthusiasm for social enterprise is particularly associated with Steve Hilton, who was until recently a close colleague and adviser of David Cameron, the present prime minister. Mr Hilton is the son of parents who left Hungary under the Communist regime and his political beliefs are deeply marked by his family's negative experience of state socialism. He has written widely about his conviction that business can be a force for good and can bring about positive social change.[1] At one time he became involved with the Green party but later returned to the Conservatives, which is in itself an interesting comment on the fluidity of formal political expression of ethical, environmentalist and social convictions in the present climate. So any group which can offer a combination of starting a business for social ends and encouraging voluntary and religious groups to deliver social services can be confident of encouragement from the present government.

In April 2012 the government announced the formation of a social enterprise bank, to be known as Big Society Capital (because 'the big society' is the government's rhetorical shorthand for a shift away from state action towards encouragement of a diversity of social actors). Its 'vision and mission' is described as being 'to develop and shape a sustainable social investment market in the UK'.[2] Although the publicity over the founding of Big Society Capital implied that it was entirely the idea of the present government, it was actually the culmination of a social enterprise initiative established by the previous Labour government in

2000 under the name of the Social Investment Task Force. The bank has been funded partly with money taken from dormant bank accounts and investments under legislation passed for the purpose in 2008, before the present government came to power. The rest of its funding comes from the so-called 'big four' banks, namely Barclays, HSBC, Lloyds and RBS. Each of these banks has given £50 million to Big Society Capital, in essence because of the government pressing them to give something back in return for taxpayer assistance during the banking crisis. This involvement of the major banks might be seen as 'contamination' by some dedicated anti-bank activists and of course purist anti-*riba* Muslims.

One of the first recipients of funding from the government social investment initiative was the Triodos New Horizons project. This is a scheme to help young people in Liverpool who are not currently in education, employment or training (NEET) to improve their skills and find work. Triodos Bank (whose work has been considered in Chapter 2, 'Retail Banking' and Chapter 3, 'Investment Funds') won a commission to undertake this work from the Department of Work and Pensions. It will be paid by results, defined as meeting pre-set targets for entry into employment and education by the young people with whom the New Horizons project works. An award of £500,000 was approved in principle in December 2011, before the formal launch of Big Society Capital. Triodos itself says that it raised £2 million for the New Horizons project 'from a syndicate of leading UK social investors including the Big Society Investment Fund' (which seems to be the name of a transitional stage between the Social Investment Task Force and Big Society Capital).[3]

This £2 million was structured as a social impact bond. The idea of such a bond is that investors will only receive a return if the project funded produces results, and that these results are defined in terms of socially beneficial outcomes. Such bonds appear to be compatible with Islamic principles as they do not guarantee any fixed payment to investors but return a profit only in relation to the success of the funded enterprise. The fact that the enterprises which the bonds fund are designed to meet social needs makes them additionally attractive to religious investors. This is an area where there is plenty of opportunity for convergence between the Islamic and the wider ethical sectors.[4]

There are eight other projects which have had funding from Big Society Capital approved to date and not all of them structure their funding in this way.[5] One of the projects is working on helping charities to issue fixed income bonds as a way of raising funds, which is obviously not compatible with Islamic principles. Charity bonds are considered in more detail in Chapter 7, 'Charities'. The organisations involved in the delivery and in the funding of social investment projects are numerous and are related to each other in complex ways, and a detailed assessment of government social investment initiatives is outside the scope of this book. One point which is relevant here is that there are political aspects to this type of social investment which may make some ethical finance enthusiasts uneasy.

The projects funded by Big Society Capital to date are very much in keeping with the government's policy of encouraging the private and voluntary sectors to deliver social services rather than leaving everything to the traditional public sector, and not all of those active in ethical or socially responsible investment are in sympathy with this policy. Triodos appears to assume that its supporters are, because it is happy to quote one of the creators of New Horizons as saying that it has shown them 'how much we can achieve with the support of the private sector'.[6] Even if social enterprise enthusiasts are happy with the involvement of a company like Triodos, they may not be so happy with some other examples of private sector involvement. A project carrying out similar work with NEET young people (Think Forward Social Impact) which has received a similar amount of funding from Big Society Capital is managed by the Private Equity Foundation. This is funded by a long list of UK private equity firms, which are detested by most ethical finance enthusiasts because private equity precludes any possibility of outside shareholders influencing the company's behaviour. This is just one example of the difficulty of reconciling a range of ethical and political policies in practice.

Islam and social enterprise

The relationship between Islamic financial models and presently fashionable models of social business is close and fruitful. Venture capital is probably the most innovative and successful area of Islamic finance in the UK at present. The *mudarabah* and *musharakah* models of business finance fit very well with modern forms of venture capital. There are no real difficulties in modernising these structures (except perhaps the principle that the *rab al-maal* bears all the losses under a *mudarabah* partnership).

The funding model known as 'peer to peer lending' has recently attracted considerable attention from financial journalists, and has clear potential for convergence with Islamic structures. The idea behind this is that those with money to invest and those who wish to borrow can be put in touch with each other directly without a bank acting as an intermediary and making large profits out of severely asymmetrical rates of interest. To date the phenomenon still involves broker intermediary companies who are also likely to be very profitable, but have been able to present this in a way which does not antagonise a public increasingly hostile to banks. The best known such broker company is Zopa. Its publicity material stresses that it is 'not a bank' and that it is making money 'human again'. To illustrate how 'human' its loans are, it provides engaging anecdotes about what its borrowers are spending their money on. This is merely clever advertising, but the fundamental concept, of savers making a return by providing assistance directly to a deserving person who will make good use of the loan, seems to be resonating strongly with the public. Funding Circle is a similar 'crowd funding' intermediary which lends to businesses rather than individuals. Both Zopa and Funding Circle are interest based lenders, with the innovative feature that they pay interest to investors at rates which vary according to how much risk the investor is willing to take. Borrowers are assessed and allocated to different risk bands, and savers choose which band they wish their money to be invested in. This model could fairly easily be adapted to a *mudarabah* structure, where investors would receive returns directly based on the success of the businesses funded rather than a fixed rate of interest. It could also be adapted to the funding of enterprises where success is defined in non-monetary terms, as with the social impact bonds described above.

In addition to Islamic religious principles there are wider cultural reasons for British Muslims from immigrant backgrounds favouring entrepreneurial models. Migrants everywhere are self-selected for being more than usually energetic, enterprising and self-reliant. The first generation of British Muslims had higher levels of self-employment than the general population.[7] Young people who have grown up in an environment of self-employment and with an awareness of the hardships which their parents overcame by hard work are more likely to be impatient with a culture of waiting for government or a large employer to create jobs and solve problems than their peers from non-migrant families.

Another factor which may become increasingly important is the changes to funding for university students. In England and Wales finance to cover tuition fees is now provided entirely in the form of interest bearing loans. (Scotland is more generous and there Scottish students do not pay their own fees.) Until recently the interest rate was set at a level no higher than inflation, which made it possible to rely on the opinion of some scholars that a rate of interest which does not increase the real value of the principal borrowed is not *riba*. The interest rate has now been increased to a level higher than inflation, though still lower than that usually obtainable on commercial loans. In addition the level of fees which universities are permitted to charge has been raised to an amount (£9,000 per year) which most students have no realistic prospect of being able to borrow from relatives. This presents a serious obstacle to obtaining a degree for devout Muslims who are not prepared to take out *riba* based finance.

The al-Qalam group of scholars, which was established to provide religious advice to British Muslims about real modern problems, has produced a *fatwa* to the effect that:

> whilst the importance of getting a university education is acknowledged, it must be maintained that it cannot be done at the expense of the prohibition on *riba*. Whilst university education is important, it is an elective lifestyle choice and one can earn a perfectly respectable livelihood without going to university.[8]

Al-Qalam is campaigning for a *Shari'ah* compliant form of finance to be offered as an alternative form of funding for students, to enable more Muslim students to go to university with a clear conscience. It is being supported in this by the Federation of Student Islamic Societies and also the National Union of Students (which is happy to embrace any argument for more advantageous terms of funding) and has been consulted on the issue by the relevant government department, which has stated that it does intend to introduce such alternative finance eventually.[9] In the meantime however it is possible that this problem may propel more British Muslims into going directly into employment or starting their own business rather than obtaining a degree.

This is an example of how exclusion from aspects of the dominant culture as a result of religious beliefs tends to drive innovation because of the need to find alternative ways of doing things. In addition to its role in personal enrichment, where an entrepreneurial culture is well established, setting up a business with a social purpose is an obvious next step.

Case studies of social financial services businesses

Fair Finance

The project known as Fair Finance is discussed here because it is a social business devoted to promoting financial inclusion. It arose from one of the largest British Muslim communities yet is not Islamic in its principles.

Faisel Rahman is a young Londoner of Bangladeshi parentage. He worked in a variety of financial institutions, including the microfinance department of the World Bank, and then for Grameen Bank, the famous pioneer of microfinance in Bangladesh. He has said that he was introduced to the founder of Grameen, which deals predominantly with female clients, by his mother.[10] He came to the controversial conclusion that the problem of lack of access to affordable credit and a resulting spiral of debt was essentially the same in the poorer parts of London as in Bangladesh and was inspired to emulate the example of Grameen in the UK. In 2005 he founded Fair Finance in East London. Mr Rahman has received a number of awards and marks of recognition for achievement in social enterprise, and for some time wrote a regular column on the subject of financial exclusion for the *Guardian* newspaper.

Fair Finance accepts clients who live or work anywhere in London but its operations are concentrated in the boroughs of Tower Hamlets, Hackney, Newham and Waltham Forest. These are the poorest boroughs of the capital and are indeed among the most deprived communities in the whole country. They also have a high percentage of Muslims among their populations: 30 per cent of the population of Tower Hamlets is of Bangladeshi origin, while 56 per cent is non-white.[11]

Fair Finance offers loans at rates calculated to make just enough profit to keep the business sustainable and it is also committed to making the terms simple to understand. In addition to offering credit it provides debt counselling and general money advice. It offers personal loans of up to £2,000 to be repaid over periods of one or two years. Repayments can be made weekly as well as monthly, which makes budgeting easier for borrowers who are paid weekly. It does require bank statements and references from 'people you have worked with' before making a lending decision but does not require applicants to be currently employed and maintains that most of those it approves for loans would have had no chance of being accepted by a conventional bank. It encourages clients to take out its loans to repay debts to other lenders whom it describes as 'predatory', in other words high interest lenders. The interest rates on personal loans are currently not advertised because they are being reviewed, but Faisal Rahman has stated that an APR of 45 per cent is necessary for the service to be sustainable. He points out that this is only one-tenth of the APR on a typical 'payday' or 'doorstep' loan.[12]

The organisation also offers business loans of up to £10,000 over five years at an interest rate of 15 to 19 per cent. It requires a business plan from applicants but will provide help to prepare one. Despite the fact that a large proportion of its clients are unemployed, Fair Finance reports that the default rate on its loans for the first three years of operation averaged only 5 per cent, which is considerably lower than the default rate of conventional bank loans.[13] It attributes this to its policy of taking the trouble to understand clients' individual circumstances in detail. It takes a relatively generous approach to default and will only begin to pursue arrears by legal means after ninety days have passed without any payment at all.

In 2010 the turnover of Fair Finance was just under £700,000 but it has recently attracted commercial funding of about £2 million from major banks, though admittedly not from British ones, which were reportedly less sympathetic, but from Santander, BNP Paribas and Société Générale. This has enabled it to expand its network of branches and to consider introducing additional services such as savings accounts.[14] This success in securing commercial support must be in part due to the relatively conciliatory attitude to the conventional banking industry which Mr Rahman has adopted. It is apparent from his writing that the real object of his ire is the non-bank high interest loan sector, and that he believes an essential part of the solution to financial exclusion to be improved practices and greater social engagement by conventional banks, which would weaken the non-bank sector's monopoly on lending to the poor.[15]

Fair Finance has adopted a commendable policy of complete transparency about its business practices and decisions, and publishes data on the recipients of all its loans from its foundation to the current month, arranged by location, gender and ethnicity. A large majority of clients are women: 71 per cent of personal loans and 61 per cent of business loans have been made to female clients. The figures on ethnicity are more ambiguous. The percentage of clients described as 'Asian' appears to be much lower than that in the population of the area, at 4 per cent of personal loans and 6 per cent of business loans. 'White' clients account for 37 per cent of personal loans but only 15 per cent of business loans (which may support the view that the non-migrant community is relatively less entrepreneurial than those from an immigrant background). 'Black Caribbean' clients received 20 per cent of personal loans and 18 per cent of business loans, while 'Black Africans' received 20 per cent of personal loans and a notable 38 per cent of business loans. A surprisingly large 20 per cent of personal loan and 22 per cent of business loan clients are ascribed to the category of 'Other' ethnicity, which confuses the overall picture. As the compilers of the 2001 national census discovered to their cost, Turks and Arabs do not identity with any of the terms Asian, White, or Black, and in London people of such origins are fairly numerous. If we assume that a significant proportion of clients of 'Other' ethnicity were Turks and Arabs, and allow that some Black Africans may be Muslim, the overall picture still suggests that Muslims are under-represented among Fair Finance clients. Certainly the figures for Asian clients are very small for an organisation based in an area which is nationally recognised for the size of its Bangladeshi community.[16]

This may be due to relative levels of deprivation, with Bangladeshi applicants more likely to be in such bad financial circumstances that even Fair Finance will not lend to them, but it is also consistent with a reluctance by Muslims to take out interest based loans. This is obviously a very sensitive area about which to enquire directly.

Zakat House

The Islamic institution of *zakat*, described in Chapter 7, 'Charities', provides a pool of money with no exact equivalent in the non-Muslim world. Although some Christians choose to pay a certain proportion of their income to their church and all religions encourage charitable giving, the status of *zakat* as one of the pillars of Islam and the precise formula employed to calculate *zakat* liability every year mean that there is a predictable amount paid every year as an obligation by all practising Muslims. As the British Muslim community matures, initiatives seeking to employ this pool of funds in the most fruitful way are beginning to appear.

Zakat House is one of these. It was founded in 2009 by Hany el-Bana, who also founded the charity Islamic Relief. The chief executive of Zakat House, Fadi Itani, was formerly the UK manager of Islamic Relief Worldwide. The aim of the project is to collect *zakat* payments from British Muslims and use them to support charities and to provide capital to new small businesses and social enterprises. It also offers a range of advice services to such organisations and makes rooms in its premises available to them for holding meetings or as permanent office space. It describes this collection of support services as forming a 'charity hub'.

The 'hub' is also the headquarters of several charities, the Humanitarian Forum, the International HIV Fund, the Muslim Charities Forum, the Somali Relief and Development Forum, and the Yemeni Relief and Development Forum. The most noteworthy of these charities is the International HIV Fund, founded in 2008, which is an interesting attempt to develop an Islamic response to the epidemic of HIV/AIDS in Africa which moves beyond simple religious disapproval of the behaviours involved in transmitting the infection.

The Zakat House project is still at an early stage and no information is available yet on particular start-up enterprises which have benefited from its support, but if it is as successful as Mr el-Bana's other foundation, Islamic Relief, it could become a significant force in the British Muslim community. The building which forms Zakat House is located in central London and was it seems 'a generous donation from people who have belief in the Zakat House project'. The identity of these supporters has not been revealed but the donation was apparently intended as *waqf*.[17] (This form of Islamic charity is considered in more detail in in Chapter 7, 'Charities'.)

Charity Bank

Charity Bank is included here because it is an unusual hybrid of social impact funding models – part charity, part bank, part public agency partnership. It also seems to suggest a shift with potential long-term cultural significance from simply donating money to charities to investing money with a view to a cash return on the investment as well as the satisfaction of helping a good cause. It is both a registered charity and a bank approved by the Financial Services Authority (FSA). It was founded in 2002, succeeding a previous organisation with similar aims called Investors in Society, which was created and initially funded by the Charities Aid Foundation.

The distinctive feature of Charity Bank is that it uses money deposited with it to lend to third sector organisations, charges the borrowers interest and then pays a return to the investor. In other words it uses the same basic model as a conventional bank except that it will only lend to groups with a social purpose and not to profit orientated businesses. It uses the word 'ethical' lavishly in its publicity material. It defines the term thus: 'ethical savings accounts means your money is used to create social impact by supporting charities, voluntary organisations and social enterprises doing good work in communities across the UK and beyond'.[18] It offers a range of savings accounts, including one for children, which pay interest rates comparable to those obtainable at present from the large banks, but not as high as those paid by some building societies. The corollary of this is that the terms given to borrowers are relatively generous. Interest rates on loans are described as being typically between 6.5 per cent and 7.5 per cent and do not vary over the course of the repayment period, because they are not linked to the Bank of England base rate. Loans start at about £50,000, repayable over five years if unsecured, or up to twenty-five years with security. This rejection of a link with the base rate is itself an interesting example to be considered in the debate over the use of bank interest.

Charity Bank reports that since its creation in 2002 it has lent about £170 million, with £105 million repaid to date and a default rate of only 0.5 per cent, and that it currently holds £65.5 million of deposits. It also points out that because it is registered and regulated by the FSA as a bank it is permitted to lend up to six times the amount of its capital and that 'our loans unlock an additional 0.5x financing for our borrowers', and that therefore 'a £250,000 capital investment results in £2.7 million in social loans to those helping the most vulnerable in society'. At first sight this appears to contrast with one of the alternative definitions of 'ethical' with wide currency at present, the version which prioritises sustainability in finance and is critical of highly leveraged lending. Of course Charity Bank is able to risk this because it is a charity as well as a bank, and is able to smooth its cash flow with the aid of outright gifts to it.

In addition to the savings of individuals who expect their safekeeping and repayment at a profit, Charity Bank also solicits donations and legacies, and furthermore it has received some large grants from a number of public and voluntary sector bodies. It has been observed in previous chapters that there is a significant clustering of alternative financial services bodies in Yorkshire. Charity Bank's head office by contrast is located in the town of Tonbridge in Kent, in the south of England. It does however have an office in York and received a grant of £10 million from the regional development agency 'Yorkshire Forward' in 2007. In the same year it received £0.5 million from the Community Foundation of Northern Ireland. Charity Bank has a Belfast office and a dedicated Northern Ireland manager, which is unusual in the world of ethical finance and probably reflects the focus on helping disadvantaged communities. It also has a manager for Wales, based in Cardiff, an office in London, and a recently appointed manager for Scotland, based in St Andrews. The organisation wishes to expand its work in Scotland but at present is not registered as a charity there.[19] (The separate system of regulation of charities in Scotland is explained in Chapter 7, 'Charities'.) It is good to see that when Charity Bank says that it works 'throughout the UK', it really means it.

The charities and voluntary organisations to which Charity Bank lends are predominantly small groups with limited and clearly defined aims and a firm base in local communities. Most of them work in fields traditionally associated with charitable activity, such as providing services to the elderly, children and people with serious health problems, improving local facilities and promoting arts and educational opportunities at a community level. There is a notable absence of 'green' organisations in the list of recipients of loans; only a small number of borrowers are classed in the 'environment' category and the majority of these are primarily concerned with creating employment through schemes which could be described as 'green'.

At the time of writing there are several churches and one Sikh temple listed as beneficiaries of the Bank's 'social impact'. All of these cases appear to have involved loans to repair and improve the premises and the emphasis is on the importance of these places of worship as community centres. (The position of religious bodies under the regulation of charities is described in in Chapter 7, 'Charities'.) It seems certain that Charity Bank would look favourably on any mosque or Muslim community group which sought assistance, but whether Muslim groups would feel comfortable about making use of such funding is another matter.

An example of a conflict of ethical policies

This story is included here as an example of a direct conflict of ethical principles arising in a social enterprise. The *Big Issue* magazine is one of the best known and most widely supported examples of a social enterprise in the UK. It was founded in 1991 to enable homeless people to earn a living from selling the magazine in public places. Subsequently it has diversified into a range of projects aimed at ameliorating poverty and deprivation, including a social investment subsidiary, Big Issue Invest.

In 2010 the directors made the controversial decision to accept commercial sponsorship of the vendors. The magazine has always included advertising, but this sponsorship arrangement involved the company supplying free high-visibility jackets for the vendors to wear, printed with the name of the magazine on the front and that of the sponsor on the back, effectively turning the vendors into walking advertisements for the sponsor in city centre locations where paid advertising spaces would have cost much more than the jackets. Some supporters felt that this in itself was demeaning to the vendors and contrary to the spirit of the magazine, but what made the decision really controversial was that the sponsor was a seller of alcoholic drinks.

Fairhills is a South African wine company which has qualified to use the 'fair trade' brand on its wine. In its promotional material it makes much of the fact that it has used the price premium which it attracts to carry out valuable development work among the communities where its employees live. This was the reason the *Big Issue* gave for regarding it as an appropriate sponsor. The question of whether it was appropriate for any alcohol producer to be promoted by vendors, particularly since drink problems are common among homeless people, was given short shrift by the magazine. Its responses to criticism never progressed beyond statements to the effect that 'no matter who it is that's sponsoring us they are helping the vendors' and 'this was something that was considered long and hard and it was decided that the positive benefits to the vendors outstripped any negatives'.[20]

The issue of whether Muslims might feel unable to wear the jackets and therefore be excluded from the opportunities offered by selling the magazine does not appear to have occurred to any of those involved in the decision and this point was never directly addressed in responses to objectors. In fact it seems likely that any Muslim vendor could make a good case for this requirement to wear the Fairhills tabard constituting indirect religious discrimination in employment. There are also some Christian groups which oppose the consumption of alcohol, and one of these is the Salvation Army, which is well known for its work with the homeless and would usually co-operate closely with the *Big Issue*. It does not seem to have made any formal statement on the sponsorship issue but it is unlikely that it approved.

This case demonstrates both the power of the 'fair trade' brand, which in the public mind now embodies all that is 'ethical', to over-ride any additional or dissenting ethical policies and the way in which a company's own image can benefit from the ethical image of a product which it sponsors. Fairhills reportedly now has the highest level of brand recognition of any 'fair trade' wine.[21]

The implications of the social enterprise sector for Islamic finance

It is becoming common for observers of the Islamic financial services industry globally to criticise the under-performance of the sector in the field of social responsibility.[22] Given the favourable climate in the UK at the present time, it seems likely that positive developments in this area will proceed faster there than in many Muslim majority countries. It could eventually be the case that successful models of Islamic social enterprise will be exported from the UK back to the Muslim majority world.

A cautionary note should however be attached to this optimistic prediction. Of all the different forms of Islamic financial activity, it is in the field of social enterprise that conflicts over principles and goals are most likely to arise. It is necessary to be very clear about what exactly the social goals of an Islamic enterprise should be and what limits to its development and to co-operation with non-Muslim partners must be set if compromises over essential Islamic principles are to be avoided.

Notes

1. Notably in: Hilton, Steve and Gibbons, Giles (2002), *Good Business*, London: Texere.

2. www.bigsocietycapital.com (accessed on 22 October 2012).

3. *The Colour of Money*, the Triodos customer newsletter, Autumn 2012, p. 15.

4. For a detailed account of Triodos social impact bonds, see 'Social impact bonds', *The Colour of Money*, Spring 2013, pp. 8–11.

5. The details of all these funding recipients and links to their own websites can be found on www.bigsocietycapital.com/how-we-invest (accessed on 26 October 2012).

6. *The Colour of Money*, Autumn 2012, p. 15.

7. Metcalf, Hilary, Modood, Tariq and Virdnee, Satnam (1996), *Asian Self-employment: The Interaction of Culture and Economics in England*, London: Policy Studies Institute.

8. Fatwa dated 20 April 2012, available on www.alqalam.org.uk/fatawa.

9. See the discussion posted on 27 July 2012 on www.media.fosis.org.uk/articles.

10. Video interview posted on www.guardian.co.uk on 3 March 2012.

11. Figures from the Office for National Statistics quoted on www.towerhamlets.gov.uk (accessed on 5 November 2012).

12. 'Banks can help the financially excluded', *Guardian*, 27 April 2011.

13. Annual report for year ended March 2008. This is the most recent report available on the website.

14. 'Microfinance entrepreneur providing affordable loans', posted on www.eastlondonlines.co.uk on 3 May 2012.

15. 'Banks can help the financially excluded', *Guardian*, 27 April 2011.

16. All of the figures in this paragraph are taken from the 'where we loan' pages on www.fairfinance.org.uk (accessed on 5

November 2012). There is a printed report of similar data available but it is much less up to date.

17. Personal communication from Mohammad Shakir, dated 20 November 2012.

18. All of the information about Charity Bank cited here is taken from www.charitybank.org (correct as of 18 November 2012).

19. Personal communication from Mark Howland, dated 19 November 2012.

20. Personal communications from Louise Woodhouse, assistant to John Bird, the editor of the Big Issue, dated 27 March 2012 and 30 March 2012.

21. www.tesco.com (accessed on 12 November 2012).

22. See, for example, Asutay, Mehmet (2012), 'Conceptualising and locating the social failure of Islamic finance: aspirations of Islamic moral economy versus the realities of Islamic finance', in *Asian and African Area Studies* 11 (2), pp. 93–113.

CHAPTER 7
CHARITIES

The recognition of some kind of moral obligation to come to the aid of those suffering from misfortune appears to be universal. All of the major religions have formalised this obligation in some way, and not only the religions of the Abrahamic tradition. Within Buddhism, for example, *dana*, generosity and giving, is the basis of all ethical behaviour and an essential step on the path to enlightenment.[1]

One of the five pillars of Islam is *zakah* (more commonly transliterated in the form *zakat*), which is the payment of one-fortieth of a person's wealth, above the amount necessary for essentials, to be spent on relieving the distress of poorer members of the community and on advancing religion and education. Islam also promotes voluntary additional charity or *sadaqah*, which is believed to incur religious merit.

Judaism requires a payment known as *tzedakah*, a Hebrew word cognate with the Arabic *sadaqah*. This is traditionally an amount of one-tenth of income and must be paid by everyone, with no minimum income before liability. It is to be spent on compassionate work among the poor, not only the Jewish poor but anyone in need of help, and may also be legitimately spent on aiding religious and educational activity. This charitable giving is regarded in Jewish tradition as one of the three acts which bring forgiveness of sins (the others being prayer and repentance).

The payment of one-tenth of income as charity is part of Christianity's inheritance from Judaism. In the Christian tradition it is known as tithing, and was a custom enforced by the church in earlier times in Britain. In this historical form it has now disappeared but the conviction that it is a religious requirement to donate one-tenth of one's income to charitable causes and to the support of churches is becoming increasingly common among newer Christian groups. More generally there is a strong encouragement of charity within all Christian denominations. This is often supported by reference to the text of St Paul which describes the foundations of the Christian life as 'faith, hope and charity' and states that 'the greatest of these is charity' (1 Corinthians 13: 13). Modern translations of the Bible prefer to translate the third of these terms as 'love', but the seventeenth-century version in which it is most familiar indicates how old and culturally resonant the word 'charity' is in Britain.

It could be argued that the use of this English word to translate the Hebrew and Arabic terminology of other religions is misleading. The root meaning of *tzedakah* and *sadaqah* is related to justice and righteousness, and that of *zakah* to purity and integrity, rather than to love or compassion. They express an obligation to preserve economic balance and social harmony through universal mutual support, rather than a permanently asymmetrical donation from rich to poor. In relation to this it is instructive to reflect that in some cultures gifts are considered to create the obligation to reciprocate and therefore can sometimes be unwelcome. The creation of obligation may be implicit in some forms of charity in cultures in which this is not explicitly recognised, such as Britain, and the potential of charitable work to be manipulative is something of which the regulators take notice.

The regulation of charities

This chapter deals not with the wider religious beliefs about charity discussed above but to the formal institution of a charity, which has a precise legal status in the United Kingdom. There are many advantages to an organisation in being registered as a charity, because charitable status confers favourable tax treatment. In particular it allows the charity to reclaim the tax notionally paid on cash donations by its supporters (the Gift Aid scheme) which can be worth a great deal of extra income. It is also generally considered that being able to demonstrate formal registration as a charity significantly enhances public trust and makes members of the public more likely to believe that the activities of the organisation are honest and legitimate and to donate to it.

Because of the privileged status of charities it is necessary to monitor their activities and to ensure that charitable registration is not being abused. The regulatory body in England and Wales is the Charity Commission. In Scotland it is the Office of the Scottish Charity Regulator. Most of the material in this chapter refers only to England and Wales.

The law relating to charities has developed piecemeal through case law over a long period, and has thus retained some historical assumptions that are no longer entirely appropriate to modern circumstances. The larger denominations of the Christian church had until recently a privileged status within the regulation of charities, but this situation has been altered by the Charities Act of 2006. This Act makes a great many provisions about the regulation and auditing of charities; it is only considered here in so far as it relates to charities with a religious purpose.[2]

In the past churches belonging to the long established and familiar denominations of Christianity qualified automatically for charitable status and did not have to apply through the usual process. This exemption has now been removed so that these churches no longer have a privileged status in relation to other religious groups. Furthermore, before the Act of 2006 religion was defined as a system of belief in 'a god' but the new legislation recognises religions which acknowledge plural gods (such as Hinduism) or no deity at all (such as Buddhism). Previously 'the advancement of religion' was accepted as a legitimate purpose for a charity, without further qualification. This dated back to a time when it was taken for granted that the religion being advanced would be Christianity, but it was also convenient for the Islamic charities which have appeared in recent times. The new legislation still recognises this as a legitimate primary purpose for a charity but states that in addition the charity must provide some tangible 'public benefit'. It is no longer possible to argue that the advancement of any religion is self-evidently a public benefit in its own right.

Some Christian groups have been alarmed by these changes and feel under attack, fearing that they cannot demonstrate what they regard as the intangible benefits of their faith in a way which will satisfy formal regulation. In practice though most religious groups engage in some form of community activity which would satisfy the 'public benefit' requirement. The assessments of particular religious groups (including Hindu and Buddhist groups) which have been undertaken so far by the Charity Commission have been notably sympathetic to the view that the promotion of the moral and ethical prescriptions of a religious belief system is in itself a public benefit.[3] An example particularly relevant here is that when assessing the Church Mission Society, the Commission considered that the promotion of ethical business practices in the places where the Society seeks converts to its faith was a clear public benefit.

The British Humanist Association (BHA) is a registered charity. It originally obtained this status on the basis of its educational work, because 'the advancement of education' has always been a recognised primary purpose for a charity. It campaigned hard during the discussion of the new Charities Act for the promotion of its anti-religious philosophical system to be recognised as a legitimate primary purpose of a charity on a par with the advancement of religion. The original name of the Association when it was founded in 1896 was the Ethical Union, and the concept of advancing a coherent ethical code of conduct remains central to the self-understanding of humanists. The BHA was unsuccessful in having humanism given parity with religious belief systems in the 2006 legislation, but subsequently convinced the Charity Commission that the omission was a contravention of the Human Rights Act, which makes discrimination on the grounds of religious belief or non-belief unlawful. After reaching an agreement with the Commission in 2011 the BHA has now adopted a new statement of its 'objects', with the primary one being 'the advancement of Humanism, namely a non-religious ethical lifestance'. The new 'public benefit' requirement is satisfied by both a continued commitment to 'the advancement of education' and by promoting such desirable ends as 'equality', 'understanding between people' and 'harmonious co-operation in society'.[4]

The decisions which the charity regulators are required to make about religious activity may appear bizarre to some non-British readers, and indeed they sometimes seem opaque even to those most familiar with Britain's particular historical culture of diverse religious proselytism and diverse forms of opposition to it. It should be stressed that this legislative and regulatory framework has important practical consequences for many groups, including some working in the financial sector. For example, the organisation Christians Against Poverty, which is discussed in Chapter 5, 'Debt and Credit', gains significant extra income from being a registered charity, and the fact that it is explicitly committed to Christian evangelism is no obstacle to this, which it would be in some other countries. Similarly, there is no problem with a charity having Islamic *da'wah* as its primary purpose, so long as it can demonstrate some other public benefit to its work. Now, following the relaxation of the definition of religion and the precedent established by the BHA, the way is open for non-monotheistic religions, 'new age' religions and formally secular groups to be given recognition by the Charity Commission and to offer public services, such as financial advice and help, from a basis of equitable tax treatment. It seems likely that this new inclusivity will cause problems at some point, and that fierce disputes over the definition and ownership of the term 'ethical' will be a prominent feature of any consequent litigation.

Some issues for Islamic charities

It has been explained above that the Charity Commission recognises 'the advancement of the Islamic faith' as a legitimate object for a charity, just as much as the advancement of Christianity, but that Islamic charities are equally bound by the requirement that their work should have public benefit beyond that of advancing the faith. This requirement can easily be satisfied by such work as providing educational facilities or visiting Muslim patients in hospital. In this respect Muslim charities in Britain are in a more fortunate position than they are in some countries where any organisation formed to promote religion, particularly Islam, is the object of suspicion by public authorities.

The publications of the Charity Commission often contain warm words about the amount of good work performed in society by faith based charities. In 2007 it established a Faith and Social Cohesion Unit. The Commission was quite open about the fact that this was conceived primarily with Muslim groups in mind, but said that the intention was to move on to work with other faith groups eventually. However, the funding it received from the Department for Communities and Local Government ended in 2010 before it could carry out any significant work with other faiths. The thinking behind the Department's funding strategy seems to have been that the strict regulations which govern registered charities offered a means of monitoring the activities of Islamic groups and deterring them from involvement in forms of political and social activity which were seen as undesirable. The Charity Commission's own statement of the Unit's aims said that it wished to encourage faith groups which would be eligible for charitable status to apply for registration with the Commission, to improve the standards of governance of such groups, and to increase the Commission's understanding of faith based organisations. It remains committed to working with groups from all faiths in this way.

The greatest challenge to registration is usually meeting the standards of transparency and accountability in the governance and finances of the charity which are required by the Charity Commission. When the Faith and Social Cohesion Unit undertook a survey in 2009 of mosques in England and Wales, 25 per cent of respondents said that they 'did not know' the annual income of the mosque.[5] There are strict requirements for financial record-keeping by charities, including the obligation to submit audited accounts annually to the Commission, which some mosque committees may have found unfamiliar. The steadily increasing numbers of mosques which are registered as charities is an aspect of the growing integration of Muslims into British society. In the assessment of the Unit's work at the time it was terminated in 2010, it reported that during its period of operation the number of mosques registered with the Commission had increased from 331 to about 650, which it regarded as a great success.[6]

The total number of Muslim charities of which the Commission was aware at that time was in the region of 1,300. The great majority of these were very small, with about half having an income of less than £10,000 per annum.[7] Only 2 per cent had an income over £1 million. There are a very small number of Islamic charities with very large turnovers. Of these by far the largest, wealthiest and best known is Islamic Relief, which is based in Birmingham but operates globally under the name Islamic Relief Worldwide. It reported an income of £82 million in 2011.[8] Muslim Aid is based in London and reported an income of £25 million in 2010.[9] The third well-known Islamic charity which works internationally is Muslim Hands, founded in Nottingham, which does not make its full accounts readily available but says that it spends about £7 million annually.[10] All of these aid organisations were originally founded in response to major humanitarian crises overseas and have since grown, developed and become increasingly similar in their operating procedures to secular and Christian aid agencies in Britain.

Charities are strictly forbidden under the terms of their registration with the Charity Commission to be politically active. Disagreements over the point when humanitarian work becomes political have occurred periodically in connection with non-Muslim charities, such as Oxfam, but

Islamic ones are especially likely to attract accusations of engaging in inappropriate political campaigning. This is notably the case in relation to relief work in the Palestinian territories, where many supporters are likely to find it difficult to see any meaningful distinction between humanitarian and political goals, and likely to be impatient with the fine detail of the Commission's restrictions. It should be reiterated here that the amount of money at stake makes it worth continuing to try to stay on the right side of this line; Muslim Hands reports that the amount of tax it has been able to reclaim on donations under the Gift Aid scheme, for which only registered charities are eligible, is sufficient to pay its entire administration costs.[11] There is also a recurrent problem of Islamic charities being accused of failing to prevent their funds being used in support of terrorism, and the Commission has undertaken several investigations into this. No currently registered charities have been found to have any direct involvement in violence but the Commission has sometimes criticised charities for inadequate record-keeping which makes it difficult to disprove such allegations decisively.

The greatest distinguishing feature of Islamic charities is the attitude which they take to *riba*, or bank interest. Both Muslim Aid and Islamic Relief run interest-free microcredit schemes as part of their development work overseas and explain that the schemes are interest-free in order to be *Shari'ah* compliant. All Muslim charities encourage supporters to donate the interest which they receive on their bank accounts to them, as a way for these supporters to rid themselves of *haraam* money. Both Muslim Aid and Muslim Hands have an option in their online donation facility to indicate that the donation is interest money, so that it can be put in a separate fund. Islamic Relief does not appear to offer this separation facility. Scholarly opinion is that because interest money is tainted by sin, it cannot be spent on the building of mosques or other purely Islamic projects, and can only be spent on relieving emergency situations. Muslim Hands explains this on its donation page.

At least as indicated by the bank branches at which these three charities state that donations to them may be made, all three charities appear to bank with one of the large conventional banks. Islamic Relief is with Barclays, Muslim Aid with Lloyds and Muslim Hands with NatWest. This must be very disappointing for the Islamic Bank of Britain, which would probably have expected to find Islamic charities among its most loyal customers. It is not clear from publically available information whether these accounts pay interest but it would be surprising if they did not. Muslim Aid explained in response to a direct enquiry that the interest on the charity's deposit account is separated from its other funds and used only to pay for emergency medical treatment essential to save lives, which is in keeping with scholarly opinion that only life-or-death emergencies can justify the use of interest money.[12] Although registered charities are required to invest their funds prudently and as far as reasonably possible maximise the return on them, the Charity Commission recognises that observing *Shari'ah* prescriptions on finance is part of the essential nature of an Islamic charity and that it would not be reasonable to require one to accept interest on funds.[13]

Islamic Relief, with by far the most money to invest, provides a detailed statement of its 'ethical investment policy'. This is very similar to the 'ethical' policies of non-Muslim investment managers. It states:

> Our investment policy is based on Islamic finance principles. Our investments will not be made in companies engaged in promoting, producing or trading in any of the following: weap-

ons, pornography, alcoholic beverages, gambling, usury or any other areas deemed as inappropriate to the vision, mission and values of Islamic Relief, as stated by the Board of Trustees.[14]

Like many organisations branded as ethical, Islamic Relief is fond of the word 'values' and its use of it here could be seen as a stylistic accommodation to the language of ethical finance. One could query whether the notion of 'values' adds anything to practices already framed by well understood religious principles.

Waqf

The institution of *waqf* is a form of Islamic charity with a long and venerated history in the Muslim majority world. It is usually translated as permanent endowment or recurring charity. If a gift is made as *waqf* it is given for a charitable purpose in perpetuity and it cannot be sold or otherwise alienated from that charitable purpose. Historically this most often took the form of gifts of land or property to be used for orphanages, hospitals, religious schools and so on. There has been much discussion about the possibilities of developing *waqf* in the United Kingdom. The concept has close similarities with the English legal concept of an endowment trust and is therefore not difficult to accommodate within English law. One problem which might arise at some point could be the question of how to ensure the supposedly infinite nature of the gift after the closure of the charity to which it was originally entrusted. An insistence that an institution can never be brought to an end is not in practice recognised by the law. (In the history of England, some supposedly perpetual institutions, such as chantries where clergy were funded to pray for the souls of the donor's relatives forever, were unceremoniously terminated when the climate of religious and legal opinion changed with the emergence of Protestantism as the majority form of Christianity.)

There is particular interest in using *waqf* to provide a secure financial base for *takaful* schemes. *Takaful* is an Islamic alternative to insurance, based on a form of mutual assurance association which should be non-profit-making with all surpluses returned to the members. So far the absence of a profit incentive has meant that few suppliers are interested in entering this market, so a scheme founded on enduring charity would have more chance of success. The problem would seem to be finding a donor prepared to donate or bequeath the substantial property that would be needed to support a viable large-scale *takaful*.

The central London offices of Zakat House (discussed in Chapter 6, 'Social Enterprise') were donated by the owner as a *waqf* for the charitable purposes in which the organisation engaged. This is an unusual example in modern Britain of the kind of direct gift of the beneficial use of a property which was a traditional form of *waqf* in the Muslim majority world.

Islamic Relief categorises a substantial proportion of its investments as *waqf*. It explains that this means it invests the capital sum and uses 80 per cent of the income for its work and 20 per cent for administrative expenses and re-investment. The rules governing its choice of investment vehicles are that they must be secure against risk and inflation, conform with Islamic principles (in other words, avoid fixed interest payments) and deliver the best return possible within the limits of the first two requirements. It seems that all of the *waqf* funds are invested in properties and the return takes the form of rent paid by commercial tenants. Islamic Relief's own head office in Birmingham was purchased partially with a donation designated as *waqf*. In this case, of course, the recurring benefit to the charity takes the form of its use of the premises rather than a cash income.[15]

Muslim Hands has produced a colourful booklet of guidance on the subject, titled *Waqf: The Modern Face of a Great Muslim Tradition*. It structures its gifts of *waqf* in the form of £550 shares in a *waqf* fund, of which £50 is an administration charge. Supporters are encouraged to buy shares in the name of someone else, which is believed to confer spiritual reward on the nominee as well as the purchaser. It promises that all investments will be entirely *Shari'ah* compliant, and in this case does deposit the funds with the Islamic Bank of Britain (IBB). It appears that the return comes from *halaal* investments made by the IBB on its behalf rather than from the purchase of property.

The Muslim Students Trust describes its ambition to institute *waqf* to provide a permanent source of support for Muslim students in Britain and Ireland.[16] At first sight this seems to be a return to a form of *waqf* familiar in the history of Muslim countries, the provision of hostels for pious students. On closer inspection however it appears that the Trust would simply use the income from investments to provide grants to students. This is typical of the type of *waqf* which exists at the present time in the UK. Several charities solicit *waqf*, and usually also refer to it as *sadaqah jariyya*, or continuing charity, to emphasise the permanence which makes it an especially useful and welcome form of contribution to their work. The way in which *waqf* operates in practice though is no different from any other long-term investment fund, except, naturally, that the investments have to be *Shari'ah* compliant. The large financial reserves of the Church of England, which only ever spends the income and never the capital and regards its endowments as being in trust for the future of the Church, are almost indistinguishable from *waqf* funds in their actual operation.

Zakat and tithing

The institution of *zakat* is one of the pillars of Islam. It takes the form of the obligatory donation of one-fortieth or 2.5 per cent of one's wealth annually to approved religious and compassionate causes. There are detailed formulae for calculating how much of one's wealth is liable to *zakat*, because there is a 'personal allowance', as it were, below which one is not liable to pay anything, and there are also different rules for different kinds of asset. So complicated can these calculations become for affluent Muslims that many Muslim accountants now offer *zakat* calculation as an additional professional service, and it is standard practice for Islamic charities to offer an automated *zakat* calculator on their websites, linked to an online donation facility. This obligation provides a large pool of funding which enables Islamic charities to carry out work on a scale which at first sight may seem disproportionate to the size of the Muslim population in the UK.

The existence of a comparable custom within Christianity is less well known by those not directly involved. Within Christian culture there is an old tradition of giving one-tenth of one's income to the church, known as 'tithing'. In Britain this historically took the form of a compulsory gift in kind of one-tenth of the produce of farming or fishing activity to the established church, which aroused a great deal of resentment among those obliged to pay it. In the industrial age this custom largely disappeared, being difficult to enforce on a mobile urban population. Most members of the older denominations of the Christian church give regular donations to the church they attend, but these do not usually amount to anything close to one-tenth of their income.

The situation is quite different among the newer

Christian groups which are now increasingly prominent in Britain, where, particularly among those who describe themselves as 'evangelical', the custom of tithing is taken very seriously as a Biblical prescription and is being re-invigorated. There are numerous references to the practice in the Old Testament, for example: 'you shall tithe all the yield of your seed that comes from the field year by year' (Deuteronomy 14: 22). The most recent survey of the habits of their members undertaken by the Evangelical Alliance found that, even though a quarter of respondents said that they had been obliged to reduce their giving because of the economic recession, the average amount given away by evangelicals every month was 11.5 per cent of household income, of which 6.5 per cent was given to their local churches and 5 per cent to Christian charities.[17] In fact some of these newer groups, who do not have the benefit of the vast reserves accumulated over the centuries by the Church of England and the Roman Catholic Church, are entirely dependent on gifts from members of the congregation to pay their ministers and to maintain or hire premises for worship.

Kingdom Bank, a Christian bank which was discussed in Chapter 2, 'Retail Banking', states that it 'recognises Bible teaching on the subject of tithing and will honour its obligations in this respect by allocating 10 per cent of Operating Profit before tax as Charitable Giving to support the growth of God's Kingdom throughout the world'.[18] Christians Against Poverty, discussed in Chapter 5, 'Debt and Credit', encourages tithing as part of its tireless efforts to solicit donations in support of its work. It is evident that any Christian charity has an incentive to promote the practice of tithing as a staple of the expression of faith, because it provides a very valuable steady supply of funds. Evangelical Christians have thus arrived independently at a system of mutual aid and a financial synergy between the advancement of their faith and their charitable work which already existed in the Muslim community.

It is tempting to speculate that the steady rise of religiously motivated self-divestment of income during a period of economic crisis is not coincidental. The imposition by religious authorities of a requirement for the rich to give a certain proportion of their wealth to help the less favoured performs a valuable role in preserving social stability. If the distribution of wealth within a community continues to become progressively more imbalanced then serious social strains develop, and if the trend is not reversed then eventually revolution results. This is probably why all religions promote charitable giving and utter warnings about the dangers of wealth unfettered by social conscience; it is an example of the role of religious faith and organisation in maintaining community cohesion. The institution of *zakat*, in particular, is an ancient example of an 'automatic stabiliser' in the economy.

In the modern multicultural society of the United Kingdom, the co-existence of these Islamic and Christian traditions has the potential to acquire a certain competitive quality. Christians could say that the one-tenth of income they give away is far more than the one-fortieth which Muslims are obliged to give. Muslims could respond that the institution of *sadaqah* or voluntary additional charitable giving sets no limit to the amount which can or should be donated.

Charity investments and fundraising

Charities have in the past sometimes been criticised for lack of concern about whether their investments were ethical, and it is true that there is always some tension between the charity's obligation to ensure the maximum return on all funds given to it and the need to avoid investing in any activities inconsistent with the spirit of its work. As with its recognition of Islamic principles, the Charity Commission recognises that ethical investment is consistent with the purposes of charities and does not impose a requirement to maximise financial returns at the expense of adhering to ethical policies. This point is given prominence in the advice to charities by the National Ethical Investment Week organisation.[19]

Naturally, all 'ethical' investment advisers and fund managers see charities as prime targets for recruitment as clients. EIRIS, the research and advisory service on responsible investment, states that one of its aims is to increase the numbers of charities observing its ethical guidelines in their investments, and to this end addresses stern warnings to charities about how much their work could be damaged by investing in ways which are perceived by supporters to be against their mission. It expresses this using the corporate language of avoiding 'reputational/stakeholder risk' and learning 'to identify factors that could be a risk to long-term financial performance'.[20]

CCLA, one of the sponsors of National Ethical Investment Week, is a fund management company which specialises in helping charities invest and claims that it manages more charity funds than any other fund manager.[21] CCLA is closely associated with the Church of England but has now expanded to handle the investments of a number of other faith groups, including some Hindu organisations. Once again though the specialist requirements of Muslim faith groups could not be handled by a non-Islamic manager, even one with expertise in faith groups and charities generally.

Investing for Good is a social investment specialist which

has received some funding from Big Society Capital. Its particular specialism is in the development of charity bonds, which are an adaptation of a conventional fixed return bond to the needs of fundraising in the voluntary sector. It describes this as using 'a well-understood and established mainstream financial product for the purposes of driving capital into the social investment market'. It is 'a standard, turnkey solution' which gives charities 'the flexibility to issue tranches of notes with different nominal amounts, maturities and coupon payments'. [22] This is another example of an impressive concentration of modish corporate jargon being applied to the unfamiliar object of charities.

Unfortunately such bonds are of no use to Islamic charities. Because all fixed interest bonds are forbidden by *Shari'ah*, the alternative instruments of *sukuk* have been developed for commercial finance in accordance with Islamic principles. The obvious next step would be for Islamic charities in the UK to issue *sukuk* for their own fundraising purposes. Only the largest such charities could cope with a *sukuk* issuance independently, but there is clearly a role for an intermediary agent specialising in this area and perhaps enabling smaller charities to hold a part share in such a scheme.

The implications of the work of Islamic charities for other forms of Islamic finance

It will be evident from this discussion that Islamic charities in the UK enjoy sympathetic treatment by the regulators and do not face any serious obstacles to their work. Indeed there is a high degree of congruence between the traditional way of thinking about charitable activity in the country and the Islamic charitable tradition.

The main challenge to Islamic charities is that of raising funds successfully without using non *Shari'ah* compliant instruments. The examples of the close relationship between secular and other faith charities and ethical investment companies indicate the scope for Islamic investment specialists to expand by advising Islamic charities.

It is in the field of charitable work that co-operation between those of different faiths is most advanced. This is particularly true in overseas aid and development work, where, for example, Islamic Relief is a member of the Disasters Emergency Committee alongside Christian Aid and the Roman Catholic CAFOD, working with the same humanitarian aims and adhering to the same code of practice. In disadvantaged communities within the UK, a common awareness of local problems is bringing faith groups together in practice, whatever the official positions of their national representative bodies may be. There is encouragement in this for the future of other forms of Islamic financial activity. With a clearer mutual understanding of common ethical goals, there is potential for co-operation between faith groups in the implementation of socially concerned financial projects.

Notes

1. Thanks to Helen Waterhouse of the Department of Religious Studies at the Open University for this information.

2. This discussion is based mostly on points raised in: 'Charities Act 2006: a guide', October 2010, and 'Charities Act 2006: public benefit and the advancement of religion', January 2010. These are briefing papers produced by Stewardship, a charity which works to facilitate fundraising for Christian purposes. They can be downloaded from www.stewardship.org.uk.

3. 'Charities Act 2006: public benefit and the advancement of religion', Appendices.

4. Personal communication from David Pollock, dated 9

November 2012, and a press release dated 13 October 2011, available on www.humanism.org.uk.

5. 'Survey of mosques in England and Wales', 2009, p. 7, a report for the Charity Commission available on www.charitycommission.gov.uk.

6. 'Faith and Social Cohesion Unit: summary of achievements and legacy', Board Paper for 21 July 2010, available on www.charitycommission.gov.uk.

7. 'Faith summary sheet: Muslim', November 2007, available on www.charitycommission.gov.uk.

8. 'Islamic Relief Worldwide Annual Report 2011', available on www.islamic-relief.org.uk.

9. 'Financial Summary 2010', available on www.muslimaid.org. The 2011 report does not seem to be available yet.

10. 'Our story' on www.muslimhands.org.uk (accessed on 19 November 2012).

11. 'How your money is spent', www.muslimhands.org.uk (accessed on 19 November 2012).

12. Personal communication from Moshiur Rahman, dated 26 November 2012.

13. Personal communication dated 1 February 2005. There is no indication that this policy has changed since then.

14. 'Islamic Relief Worldwide Annual Report 2011', p. 30.

15. 'Islamic Relief Worldwide Annual Report 2011', p. 29.

16. www.msconline.org.uk (accessed on 19 November 2012).

17. Press release from the Evangelical Alliance, dated 23 June 2010, available on www.eauk.org.

18. 'Charitable giving policy' on www.kingdombank.co.uk (accessed on 18 November 2012). The somewhat eccentric capitalisation is in the original.

19. 'Charities and churches – sustainable returns', on www.neiw.org (accessed on 19 November 2012).

20. 'The case for responsible investment', on www.eiris.org (accessed on 19 November 2012).

21. www.ccla.co.uk (accessed on 19 November 2012).
22. www.investingforgood.co.uk/charity-bonds (accessed on 19 November 2012).

CHAPTER 8

THE CONCERNED CONSUMER

In the real lives of individuals, the distinction between the use of financial services and other forms of retail consumption is not a rigid one. Those who care about the ethical credentials of their financial providers usually display the same concern about the suppliers of the goods on which they spend their money. This chapter moves beyond the field of financial services to consider the wider phenomenon of the emergence of a concerned consumer and the relationship between Islamic and 'ethical' customer behaviour in the general consumption of goods and services.

The Islamic shopper

In the immediate aftermath of the terrorist attacks of 11 September 2001 a shocked British media produced extensive coverage of the British Muslim community in an attempt to understand lives in which it had taken little interest before. One such article appeared to seek to reassure its readers that British Muslim women were far more interested in shopping for clothes than in politics. The lady profiled in the piece said that she loved fashion and the fact she chose to observe *hijab* and always cover her head with a scarf was in no way inconsistent with this. In fact, she owned 'more than 150 different scarves'.[1] At that time the existence of an Islamic consumer was barely recognised. There was still a widespread assumption that religious observance was incompatible with modernity and certainly with conspicuous consumption. Some Muslim writers shared this view. Aziz Al-Azmeh once illustrated a contrast between Islam and modernity by saying 'a black headscarf is not a fashion statement', assuming that this was self-evident.[2] Nowadays it is entirely possible for a black headscarf to be a fashion statement, if it is printed with the name of a celebrity designer. Indeed in some contexts this type of high fashion *hijab* functions as the symbol of modernity in contrast with the traditional dress of Muslim majority countries.

The Islamic consumer is now being actively targeted by many companies. Some of the world's largest nations and fastest growing economies are majority Muslim, and most Muslim majority countries also have much younger demographics than Western nations. The prospect of securing brand loyalty from millions of young people with rapidly rising standards of living has prompted a growing number of marketing departments to advertise their products as *halaal* or 'Muslim friendly'. The phenomenon has generated both academic conferences and coverage in the mainstream media.[3]

Probably the most significant indication of the importance of this market sector to have appeared in the UK is the decision by the Ogilvy & Mather advertising agency to set up a *halaal* branch. This was launched in 2010 under the name Ogilvy Noor. (*Noor* is the Arabic for 'light' and is a favourite name for all manner of Islamic products and services.) It describes itself as 'the world's first bespoke Islamic branding practice' and claims to be able to offer a truly global service by taking advantage of the existing international network of Ogilvy & Mather offices. It has dedicated representatives for Europe, North America, the Middle East and North Africa, South East Asia and South Asia. It gives prominence in its publicity material to the fact that the Muslim population worldwide is 1.8 billion and the claim that the *haalal* market is worth $2.1 trillion and growing at $500 billion year. There must of course be a question about to what extent Muslims care that their purchases are *halaal* or are branded as *halaal* and therefore how much extra business can be created by Islamic branding. Ogilvy Noor reports that 90 per cent of Muslims questioned say that their faith influences their purchasing decisions but the agency believes there is a question over the 'elasticity of the Islamic premium', in other words how much more customers are prepared to pay for religiously compliant products. Overly optimistic predictions of the size of this premium have been among the reasons for the performance of the Islamic financial sector in the UK having been disappointing in comparison with initial expectations, and it is possible that the current hopes for the wider Islamic market may also prove to have been exaggerated. The size of the market for *Shariʻah* compliant products is not necessarily the same as the size of the Muslim population.

The Ogilvy Noor representative for Europe is Shelina Janmohamed, whose profile states that 'with her unique British-Muslim perspective and commercial background she hopes to increase understanding and awareness of Muslim consumers and their increasing importance in today's world'.[4] Ms Janmohamed has expressed the opinion that Muslims are in the forefront of concerned consumers who want to know the whole story about the products they buy.[5] They are no longer satisfied to accept certification by a regulatory body as a guarantee that a product is *halaal*, they actively investigate a company's claims to compliance for themselves, and in some cases have not been satisfied that products certified as *halaal* truly are so. In early 2013 there was a major scandal in the UK over mis-labelling of meat products which demonstrated the legitimacy of these concerns. While the general public was mostly concerned about horse meat being passed off as beef, food testing agencies also found a number of instances of pork being present in products marketed as *halaal.*

In this way Muslim consumers are very much in line with the wider trend for conscious purchasing behaviour, for active engagement with the whole history of a product or service before a decision to purchase is made. These concerns are crystallising around the concept of *tayyib*, which Islamic branding experts believe is a step beyond *halaal* and will become the new stamp of Islamic approval. *Tayyib* is an Arabic word meaning 'good' in a comprehensive sense. In this marketing context it is usually translated as 'wholesome'. If a product is accepted as *tayyib* it has satisfied Muslim customers of its religious compliance, purity and integrity throughout the manufacturing and sales process. This term could usefully be adopted by the secular ethical consumer movement, as it seems to express very succinctly a whole range of concerns that much writing by secular activists struggles to articulate over many pages. (In lieu of this the word 'sustainable' seems to be starting to take on a similar meaning of 'entirely good and acceptable'.)

There are though a number of tensions between Islamic consumerism and other areas of the ethical consumer movement, notably the type of environmentalism which employs the slogan 'reduce, reuse, recycle' to sum up its rejection of what it sees as an excessive love of shopping in modern society. Muslims are becoming aware of their power to influence society through their consumption choices. Their purchasing power is the ultimate assurance that their views will be respected and their religious concerns accommodated. This influence can only be exercised by continuing to consume. To voluntarily reduce the amount of shopping they do would be to reduce the influence they can have on the development of society. The type of approach to ethical consumption which condemns all purchases beyond what is essential for life as frivolous and calls for voluntary simplicity, even austerity, of lifestyle as the only way to 'save' the planet or humanity cannot easily be reconciled with the promotion of Islamic branding.

The approbation of austerity is characteristic of much Christian thinking on financial and economic matters, which never quite seems directly to address the problem called by economists 'the paradox of thrift', that is, that reduction of consumption increases unemployment by putting those who manufacture and sell the spurned goods out of business. I argue below that the anti-consumer form of environmentalist activism is strongly influenced by this strand of the Christian tradition. There are also some Islamic thinkers who are critical of the very concept of the *halaal* consumer and see excessive consumption as intrinsically un-Islamic.

There is however another version of the ethical consumer movement which also sees the influence gained by purchasing power as essential for bringing about change. Since it is much easier to recruit people to a version of activism which takes the form of consuming conscientiously than to one which urges the renunciation of consumption, and since by definition providers of goods and services do not need to take any notice of people who have announced that they have no intention of buying their products, it is this type of customer who has influence. It is also this type of consumer who may well increasingly converge with the Islamic consumer.

A recent article by the editor of *Emel* magazine, a Muslim

lifestyle magazine in which a great deal of Islamic branding is featured, rehearsed the familiar regrets that shopping
malls are now being built on a scale of grandeur reserved
in the past for religious buildings, and argued that to guard
against the danger of making a religion out of shopping we
should make sure that our faith is as much part of our activity in these modern day cathedrals or mosques as in any
other aspect of our lives: 'Our purchasing decisions can be a
yielding of our incomes to the will of the Merciful [Allah]'.
Sarah Joseph summed up with the snappy sentiment: 'We
have to take our faith with us to the shopping mall, in order
to ensure the shopping mall doesn't become our faith'.[6] This
sentence would meet with the entire approval of Christians
and most secular ethical activists as well as Muslims.

Islamic environmentalism

We have seen that throughout the self-described 'ethical'
sector, environmental considerations feature very prominently indeed. In some promotional material the word
ethical is used as almost synonymous with 'green'. So in
discussing the attempts of the providers of Islamic goods
and services to position them within the ethical sector, it is
necessary to consider the relationship between Islam and
the modern environmentalist movement. Because green is
the traditional colour of Islam, references to 'green Islam'
soon become confusing, but this coincidence can also make
an association between Islam and environmentalism seem
inevitable.

It has become commonplace to describe the modern
environmentalist movement as resembling a religious faith.
In so far as this is so, it is predominantly Christianity which
it resembles. One author[7] has taken this further and argued
that American environmental activism is a development of

that country's Protestant heritage, which is an intriguing variation on Weber's famous thesis about the relationship between Protestantism and capitalism. Be that as it may, it does seem to be possible to discern a conceptual scheme in much 'green' rhetoric which is distinctively Christian. In this version of environmentalism the emphasis is on the need for greater austerity of lifestyle, reduced consumption and individual self-denial as the only way to 'save the planet'. Suggestions of technological innovations which might, for example, be able to reduce or reverse global warming without the need for a reduction in economic activity are usually dismissed impatiently by this type of activist, for whom the reduction in consumption appears almost to be an end in itself. The heavy use of the term 'save', often with no clear definition, is very reminiscent of its use within traditional Christian doctrine.

So Muslims living as minorities in Christian heritage countries such as the UK who are interested in environmental issues find themselves confronted with a form of discourse heavily coloured by a religious tradition which is not their own. There are also significant cultural reasons for the lack of interest in the environment typically shown by the first generation of Muslim migrants to the UK. The majority of them came from poor rural communities in Pakistan and Bangladesh where agricultural labour was an unpleasant lifestyle which they wished to escape. The idea of cultivating a garden for pleasure was incomprehensible to them and indeed their lack of interest in maintaining the gardens of their houses was often a source of friction with neighbours.[8] There are signs that attitudes are changing. In recent times there have been some successful projects which have invoked the historical tradition of Islamic gardens as a way of interesting British Muslims, particularly women, in improving the physical environment of their communities.[9]

While older British Muslims may not take much interest in issues such as climate change in the abstract, they do usually take a close interest in events in their countries of origin, so the fact that Bangladesh is one of the countries which will be most severely affected by rising sea levels as a result of global warming, and already suffers from frequent flooding, is obviously of concern to the large number of British citizens of Bangladeshi origin.

The development of systematic Islamic scholarship on environmental issues is a fairly recent development and it is still an area relatively neglected by researchers within the field of Islamic studies. There are many passages of the Quran which express reverence for the beauty and wonder of the creation, sometimes with the additional observation that 'in this there are signs for people who take thought' (for example 13: 3). The deduction that God intends us to study and learn from nature follows easily from this.

The foundation of Islamic environmentalism is the concept of *tawhid*, which is in fact the central concept of Islam. It means 'one-ness' or 'unity', and refers to the absolute unity and uniqueness of God. Although Islam also insists on the complete separation between the Creator and his creation (in distinction to the Christian doctrine of the Incarnation), some scholars argue that the creation shares the nature of the Creator and therefore naturally exists in a state of perfect unity, harmony and balance (*mizan*). In fact the world exists naturally in a state of perfect submission to God, which is what Islam means. Only human beings were given free will and are therefore capable of rebelling against God and disturbing this state of natural Islam. The scholarship of Islamic environmentalism begins from the belief that it is our religious duty to strive to restore this state of harmony in the world and to keep the world the way God is presumed to want it, since it is how he chose to create it.[10]

Some writers on Islamic finance also use the concept of *tawhid* as the basis for the argument that any financial system which does not tend to promote social harmony falls short of the Islamic ideal. Writers on both Islamic finance and Islamic environmentalism sometimes seem to struggle to express verbally the profound ideal of harmony which motivates them. The same is true of some non-Muslim activists in the financial and environmental fields, such as those who became involved in the Occupy movement. The inspiration of such protesters is often dismissed as purely emotional, but it may be truer in some cases to say that they have a concept of unity and harmony in the world which is not easy to express in conventional political terms.

The second key concept in Islamic 'green' thought is that while the whole of creation self-evidently belongs to God, he has appointed humanity to be his *khalifa* or regent on earth. This is the same word which has come into English in the form 'caliph' but in this context it is usually translated as guardian or steward, in which form it fits in very neatly with the concept of stewardship of the natural world commonly found in environmentalist writings.

The most prominent advocate of this concept of stewardship and of Islamic environmentalism generally in the UK at the present time is Fazlun Khalid, the director of the Islamic Foundation for Ecology and Environmental Sciences (IFEES). He founded IFEES in 1994 but its newsletter *Eco Islam* has only been published since 2006. Although Mr Khalid himself belongs to an older generation of British Muslims (he was born in 1932 and only became seriously interested in environmental issues after his retirement), his work is an important influence on young activists.

To summarise then, there is now a generation of British Muslims who have grown up in a world far removed from subsistence farming and some of whom have a reverence for the natural environment close to that typical of much of British society as a whole but increasingly presented in Islamic terms. Believing that concern for the environment is at the heart of Islam, they have joined the ranks of 'green' consumers.[11] The generational division in attitudes on this subject suggests that such concerns will become a more important aspect of marketing to Muslims in future, and that Islamic financial service providers will increasingly need to take account of them.

Ethical and *halaal*

The starting point for the discussion in this section was an advertising slogan used by a certain shop which made much of how 'green' it was. Its advertising material proclaimed that everything it stocked was 'organic, local and fair trade' and that therefore shopping with it was '100 per cent ethical'. This is a good example of the way that the term 'ethical' has become so over-used in advertising that it is in danger of losing any meaning. It is important to analyse such claims if we are to keep hold of a meaningful conceptualisation of ethics in business.

In the first place, the implication that all the other shops in town are somehow unethical must be viewed as problematic. The use of 'ethical' as a form of branding inevitably casts this slur on competitors, which, while it may be an effective marketing strategy, cannot be accepted uncritically by those with a serious philosophical or religious commitment to particular ethical standpoints.

Although there are occasional examples of British Muslims, usually younger ones, expressing interest in organic food production, for Muslims the issue of over-riding concern with food products is of course that they are *halaal*, and everything else is secondary to that. The campaign for the easy availability of *halaal* meat was the main issue on which the first generation of Muslim immigrants to Britain organised as Muslims, and it is a struggle that has been very successful. Animal welfare is a very sensitive issue for British Muslims, because there is a long history of opposition to *halaal* slaughter being expressed as if it were solely an animal welfare issue while being used as cover for a generalised attack on any concessions to Muslim culture being made within British society. So while some individual Muslims may well care that the meat they purchase comes from animals that have been reared in humane conditions,[12] it is unlikely that this issue will be explicitly adopted as part of an Islamic consumer agenda.

A little known aspect of the controversy about *halaal* meat is that Muslims in Britain are heavily over-represented among purchasers of lamb. They eat about 20 per cent of all the lamb produced in the UK, although they are only 3 per cent of the population.[13] This is partly because they do not, of course, eat pork, partly because there are relatively few vegetarian Muslims, and partly because of the custom of purchasing a sheep or goat to sacrifice at celebrations, particularly at Eid al-Adha but also in some cases at private family celebrations. British farmers also export a large amount of sheep meat to Muslim majority countries, particularly in the Gulf. The *halaal* market is very important for the British sheep raising industry, so much so that the industry marketing body has put considerable effort into researching the issues surrounding religious slaughter and into informing and reassuring Muslim customers about the *halaal* standards of the meat they purchase. Some non-Muslim 'ethical' consumers, who are likely in principle to support 'multiculturalism', are nevertheless sincerely convinced that *halaal* slaughter is cruel and may therefore regard it as actively unethical. Animal welfare activists who chose to target farmers supplying the *halaal* market could cause significant disruption of meat supplies for Muslims and create an atmosphere of distrust which could hinder the convergence of the Islamic and ethical consumer markets for a long time.

The elevation of locally produced food to automatic 'ethical' status is problematic for a community of immigrant origin who favour a cuisine relying on many imported ingredients.[14] At the present time there is clearly evident within some sections of the ethical consumer movement a localist agenda, particularly with reference to food, and a commitment to British farming which goes beyond a concern for equitable treatment of food suppliers to the identification of farming and landscape as embodiments of heritage and culture. Even the Church of England came out with such a statement in the foreword to an otherwise very thoughtful study of the treatment of farmers by supermarkets: 'The link with the land, which is a powerful theme in theology, scripture and folk-lore, may well be lost and with it an essential part of our national heritage and identity'.[15] This localist movement sometimes seems to contain elements of what anthropologists refer to as nativism, that is a rejection of anything perceived as foreign and an attribution of worthiness to anything perceived as a product of an authentic, indigenous culture. This must make people of immigrant heritage feel uneasy, as the potential of such a movement to be annexed to a xenophobic political campaign is obvious.

The debate on the economic and social benefits of aiming for local self-sufficiency versus encouraging international specialisation in trade is very complex and cannot be considered in detail here. The important aspect of it for this book is that automatically regarding local supply as desirable ignores the great benefits which migrant communities have obtained from the transnational networks of which they are a part. The traditional political arguments about immigration involved controversies over whether immigrants should assimilate entirely with their host society in language and culture and whether they could ever be trusted to be loyal to their new country and no other. This is a debate which has been overtaken by the phenomenon of globalisation, although some politicians and academics appear not to have noticed. In the new world order and the globalised economy those with transnational contacts and the ability to speak several languages possess great advantages. This point is emphasised by those working in Islamic branding. Ogilvy Noor maintains that there is now a transnational Muslim identity, that Muslims everywhere have shared values and concerns arising from their faith and that these can be targeted by international branding and advertising campaigns. There is thus a disjunction between the marketers and those who still argue about whether or not British Muslims are really British. The emergence of an Islamic financial services industry which is truly international is the most prominent illustration of this. Finance is the most global of industries and Islam is, we are often told by Muslim scholars, the most global of religions. The implications of this for the attempt to position Islamic finance within the ethical sector are not entirely clear yet.

This leads on to the issue of 'fair trade'. This is a movement which aims to promote development in poor countries largely dependent on producing primary commodities by guaranteeing a minimum price for such commodities regardless of market fluctuations and helping the producers to use this extra income to fund community infrastructure projects. Goods branded as 'fair trade' are now a significant retail sector and the principle enjoys almost universal public support, even if not everyone is prepared to pay the price premium to express support in practice. The celebrated

Muslim writer Tariq Ramadan once recommended that Muslims should become involved in the 'fair trade' movement, because the values of justice in international trade were very much in accordance with Islamic values.[16] This is certainly true and any commitment by 'concerned consumers' to equitable trade arrangements can easily be adopted by Islamic consumers. The only criticism of this movement usually heard in the UK is muted comment about market distortions from purist supporters of free trade.

Ethical consumers in Britain are on the whole unfamiliar with the viewpoint most forcefully expressed by Vali Nasr, who has produced a powerful argument for unrestricted capitalism being the most progressive force in the Muslim world.[17] For those living under oppressive regimes which attempt to control the economy for their own benefit, what they long for is not something defined by outsiders as 'fair trade' but simply the freedom to engage in any trade they choose and to retain the fairly acquired profits. Nasr provides detailed examples of how the imperatives of trade are working to undermine such regimes in several countries, with particular emphasis on his native Iran. It follows from this argument that Nasr is vehemently opposed to the use of economic sanctions as a political tool against regimes regarded as unacceptable by the governments imposing the sanctions, notably that of the United States where he now lives. He believes that far from undermining the objectionable governments, sanctions actually both alienate and weaken the most progressive forces in society, namely the activities of the business class.

This is a view not commonly found among non-Muslim concerned consumers in Britain. The origins of the ethical consumer movement, in Britain and Ireland at least, lie in the campaign to boycott goods produced in South Africa while the apartheid regime was still in existence. This was the first large-scale and widely supported attempt to use purchasing choices to bring about a political aim. The evidence about how far the consumer boycott helped to hasten the end of apartheid is mixed and still disputed. What is not disputed is the legacy it has left in the popular imagination, which retains a firm conviction that if one dislikes the present government of a nation it is logical to avoid buying goods produced there. The example particularly relevant to Muslims is that of Israel, which is considered below.

True economic liberals of the Nasr type are not that common in British politics. The most highly placed example in the present government is probably Vince Cable, who retains an unfashionable belief that economic globalisation and free trade have done more good than harm. He is opposed to protectionism in all its forms and is well aware of the sort of trade protectionism disguised as environmental concern which is sometimes referred to as 'greenwash'. This has led him to an even more unfashionable criticism of those movements which are increasingly being depicted as the virtuous opponents of the dark forces which brought about the banking crisis and the economic recession:

> The radical extremes of the 'green' movement or the 'anti-globalization' left, and some of the religious and ethical critics, never had any faith in the private enterprise system and want to see it ripped down (though the nature of their alternative is usually unclear or deeply unappealing).[18]

Such a challenge to a range of concerned consumers to consider whether their approach is the only ethical one deserves to be heard more often. For the Islamic consumer the issues involved are even more complex. Does the attempt to position the Islamic sector in finance and retail within the British ethical sector entail a risk of sacrificing an alternative vision of what ethical means? Might Muslims in less developed countries feel that their British brothers and sisters have been too much influenced by the self-indulgent post-scarcity culture of a rich society?

The boycott of Israel

Although it would not generally be included in a discussion of ethical consumerism, the issue of the boycotting of Israeli goods is included here because it illustrates in a particularly stark form some of the problems in reaching a generally accepted definition of what ethical, or more realistically unethical, really means. The majority of Muslims are hostile to Israel and many non-Muslims, while often reluctant to oppose Israel outright because of a consciousness of the European history of anti-semitism, are sympathetic to the Palestinian cause. There are several organisations campaigning for a total boycott of all goods produced in Israel and this issue sometimes arises in discussions of ethical consumerism. The most prominent of these initiatives is the Boycott Israeli Goods movement associated with the Palestine Solidarity Campaign (PSC). There is a discussion of these organisations on the *Ethical Consumer* website which, while it complains of difficulty in obtaining up-to-date lists of which companies to target, is entirely sympathetic in tone.[19]

The Co-operative Group explicitly positions itself as an ethical company and this applies to the supermarket division of the group just as much as the banking division (which was discussed in Chapter 2, 'Retail Banking'). It sells a large proportion of 'fair trade' goods and makes heavy reference to its ethical sourcing policies in its advertising material. In April 2012 it announced that as part of this policy of selling only ethically supplied goods it would no longer stock items produced by a number of companies associated with Israeli settlements regarded as having been established in violation of international law.

This decision was hailed as a 'historic and welcome decision' by the Palestine Solidarity Campaign in the UK. The PSC chose to regard the Co-operative's decision as the result of its own campaigning and interpreted it as an 'important advance' towards the 'complete boycott of all Israeli companies' which it wants to see and which is how it interprets an ethical trading policy in this matter.[20] In fact the supermarket's policy is based on a much narrower and more closely argued position, namely that it will not buy from an area 'where there is international consensus that the status of a designated region or state is illegal'.[21] The only two examples of this at present, it says, are the Israeli Occupied Territories and the Moroccan settlements in Western Sahara. The pre-1967 borders of Israel are regarded as legitimate by international bodies and so the Co-operative will buy from companies within them. This will not please most Palestinian activists. On the other hand refusing to buy from companies based in the West Bank will probably lead to the Co-operative in its turn being boycotted by groups and individuals supportive of Israel. This is the kind of controversy which arises when a company tries to base its ethical policies on precise definitions and not merely warm-hearted rhetoric.

EIRIS, the research and advisory service on responsible investment, recently produced an article on the progress of ethical investment in Israel. It found regrettably little awareness of the principles of socially responsible investment among Israeli companies and little demand from Israeli consumers for companies to take more account of environmental and social impact. On the face of it this may offer self-consciously ethical investors overseas a reason to avoid Israeli companies without having to make difficult political decisions. The writers of the report found that the only Israeli funds which did take account of environmental and social concerns were those managed in accordance with Jewish law and certified as religiously compliant by rabbinical councils. This presumably presents a dilemma for the secular Israeli environmentalist. The example of Israel has lessons for ethical investors everywhere, in as much as it demonstrates that in reality ethical issues are complex and multi-faceted and require investors to make decisions on which issue is most important to them.[22]

In 2009 the US company General Electric issued a *sukuk* which was sold internationally and sought to attract Middle East investors. This was the first American *sukuk* issuance and it caused some excitement in Islamic financial circles. It therefore comes as a surprise to find General Electric included by the US Palestine Solidarity Committee in a list of companies which should be boycotted by pro-Palestinian activists because it is a supplier to the Israeli military.[23] (The exclusion of arms manufacturers from most Islamic investment funds, officially for the same humanitarian reasons as secular funds give for excluding them, serves the additional purpose of avoiding any exposure to the large Israeli arms industry.)

This problem of which principle to prioritise – religious support for *Shari'ah* compliant finance or political support for Palestinians – could easily be replicated in relation to a British company as Islamic financial instruments become more widely used in the UK. The bigger question of whether consumer boycotts have any positive effects anyway, considered above, is likely to be raised in relation to this intensely emotive geopolitical dispute only after it has become an acceptable discussion topic among non-Muslim concerned consumers, and even that seems still some way off.

The implications of the wider ethical consumer movement for the Islamic sector

The most interesting fact to emerge from this discussion of the relationship between the Islamic consumer and other kinds of 'ethical' consumer is that in this area Muslims may be leading the way. The imperatives of religious prescription are propelling them into taking an active interest in every stage of the production and sale of products which they are considering purchasing, and influencing the forms of marketing and advertising used to target Muslims. While many non-Muslims take an interest in some ethical aspects of their purchases, not many appear to display a similar dedication to learning about the entirety of the production and sale of an item. The commonest kind of secular ethical concern driving such dedication is food related, connected to vegetarianism or commitment to organic farming or animal welfare. While this is an area where Muslim and secular preferences may clash directly, there are also reports that the rigorous standards for certification of ingredients required to label cosmetics and toiletries as *halaal* are attracting non-Muslims who are committed to avoiding animal products.[24] This is suggestive of possible future convergences which would deepen the concepts of goodness and purity which underlie the term *halaal* and develop it in a way which could be embraced by non-Muslims.

Notes
1. 'Mrs Islam – modern Muslim', *Daily Telegraph*, 15 November 2001.
2. Al-Azmeh, Aziz (1993), *Islams and Modernities*, London: Verso, p. 6.
3. For example, *The Future is Halal*, broadcast on BBC Radio 4 on 21 August 2012.

4. www.ogilvynoor.com/about-us (accessed on 10 October 2012).

5. Shelina Janmohamed expressed these views in the Radio 4 programme cited above, in note 3, and confirmed them in a personal conversation on 12 October 2012. I am grateful to her for making me aware of the concept of *tayyib*.

6. Joseph, Sarah (2012), 'Cathedrals of consumerism', *Emel* magazine, October.

7. Dunlap, Thomas R. (2004), *Faith in Nature: Environmentalism as Religious Quest*, Seattle: University of Washington.

8. Gilliat-Ray, Sophie and Bryant, Mark (2011), 'Are British Muslims "Green"? An overview of environmental activism among Muslims in Britain', *Journal for the Study of Religion, Nature and Culture*, vol. 5.3, pp. 284–306.

9. Dehanas, Daniel Nilsson (2010), 'Broadcasting green: grassroots environmentalism on Muslim women's radio', *Sociological Review*, 57.2, pp. 141–55.

10. This summary is based on Gilliat-Ray and Bryant (2011), Dehanas (2010), and material in *Eco Islam*, available on www. ifees.org.

11. Personal conversation with Arwa Aburawa on 9 January 2012.

12. See, for example, Fazila Bux (2012), 'Animal welfare and Muslims', *Asian Image*, 9 March 2012, available at www.asian-image.co.uk.

13. Eblex, *The Halal Meat Market*, p. 3. Eblex is the marketing body for English sheep and beef farmers. This report is undated but includes data up to 2008. It is available on www. eblex.org.uk.

14. This view was put forward in Alibhai-Brown, Yasmin (2010), 'Think local, eat global', *The Independent*, 7 December.

15. Church of England Ethical Investment Advisory Group (2007), *Fairtrade Begins at Home: Supermarkets and the Effect on British Farming Livelihoods*, November, p. 7.

16. Ramadan, Tariq (2004), *Western Muslims and the Future of Islam*, Oxford: Oxford University Press, p. 173.

17. Nasr, Vali (2010), *The Rise of Islamic Capitalism*, New York: Free Press. This book was previously published under the title *Forces of Fortune.*

18. Cable, Vince (2009), *The Storm*, London: Atlantic Books, p. 117.

19. www.ethicalconsumer.org (accessed at 2 October 2012).

20. Newsletter of the Newcastle upon Tyne branch of the Palestine Solidarity Campaign, dated 4 May 2012.

21. Co-operative Group, *Our Stand On Human Rights*, p. 6. Available at www.co-operative.coop (accessed on 2 October 2012).

22. Levtzion-Nadan, Noga, and Lubensky, Jonathan Porat, 'The key role that responsible investors play in driving corporate ESG performance in Israel', www.eiris.org, 3 October 2012. This paper is available on the Eiris website or from the authors' company Greeneye, www.greeneye.co.il.

23. www.palestineinformation.org (accessed on 2 October 2012).

24. Personal conversation with Shelina Janmohamed, 12 October 2012.

CONCLUSION

Some difficulties with the term 'ethical'

The difficulty which emerges most clearly from the case studies in this book is that the ethical finance industry assumes a consensus on what constitutes ethical finance or ethical consumption more generally. Such a consensus does not in fact exist. In most cases the promoters of products branded as 'ethical' appear themselves to be unaware of the contradictions and inconsistencies. It does not however follow from this that a standardisation of the term would be desirable, even though the financial services industry would very much like the term 'ethical' to be standardised. It is a complaint often heard from fund managers, for example, that the ethical sector has not developed to its full potential because the lack of standardisation makes marketing difficult. If too much weight is given to the requirements of marketing, this risks turning the term 'ethical' into nothing more than a label. This would close down a legitimate debate on which practices are unethical, in the same way as the debate on what constitutes fairness in trade arguably has been closed down by the invention of a 'fair trade' brand name.

Some providers in the ethical sector use the language of

morality inappropriately, presenting consumption choices as moral decisions when in fact customers with differing views on economic or scientific issues could arrive at different conclusions from equally well intentioned starting points. It is particularly the environmentalist elements of the ethical sector that use an over-moralistic language to address their potential customers. Climate change is largely a practical problem demanding a technological solution. It is not appropriate to talk as if our response to it were a moral issue of the same quality as the fundamental precepts of the major religions.

Part of the problem is that the secular ethical sector lacks a reference point for its own ethical standards. The Christian churches like to say that the humanitarian concerns of those who describe themselves as non-religious are in reality derived from the Christian inheritance which they have rejected at a conscious level. In Britain this is true to a considerable extent. There is however growing research evidence that the most fundamental moral concerns are common to all cultures and may be an inherent part of the evolution of human society. Those who believe that there is an irreducible core of moral standards shared by all religions and societies need to make this more explicit and appeal to such a position more deliberately in their promotional materials.

A large part of the appeal of ethical products is to those who like to 'make up their own minds' about what is right or wrong and not just accept opinions received from religion or the wider society. This is appropriate up to a point but the over-emphasis on individual opinion in the promotion of ethical products has led to the inconsistencies and confusion which are such a marked feature of the field. In reality the individual consumer's choices are strongly influenced by fashion and by peer opinion. There is nothing intrinsically wrong with this but to confuse it with taking a principled stand is dangerous. It risks stigmatising those who take a different view as not merely unfashionable but immoral. There is an argument that employing the marketing technique of making customers who reject your products feel they are unethical is in itself ethically dubious.

This is why the term 'concerned consumer' seems preferable to 'ethical consumer'. This recognises the existence of a growing body of consumers who have a social conscience and an enquiring mind and want to know as much as possible about how products are made and what effects they have in the course of their production, use and disposal. It does not make inappropriate and misleading judgements about which of these concerned citizens are 'ethical' and which are not.

Niche brand or radical reform movement

Ethical products are often more expensive than the alternatives. This may take the form of a higher purchase price for a commodity or a lower return on an investment. Quite often the sellers will acknowledge this but present it in a positive way, positioning their products as something which costs more but does more good. Customers are made to feel that they are prepared to pay more to do good, and this makes them feel good about themselves. There is an element of 'showing off' in such consumption choices. In Britain today ostentatious luxury is considered unacceptable or at least vulgar in many social circles, but the display of goods which are known only by one's well informed peer group to be more expensive sends a subtle message of affluence. This is sometimes referred to by economists as the Veblen effect, after the economist who first described the phenomenon. The promotion of organic baby clothes and boutique artisan cheese as being necessarily expensive because they are ethical carries an unmistakable suggestion that 'ethical' purchases may also be 'Veblen goods'.

The same phenomenon may exist in the Islamic sector to some extent. We have seen, in the chapter on *The Concerned Consumer*, that there is uncertainty in the advertising industry over 'the elasticity of the Islamic premium'. On the other hand, the fact that, before the anomaly was removed by legislation, Islamic house purchase models were known to be significantly more expensive than conventional finance may actually have been an added attraction to a certain type of purchaser. Looked at this way, well intentioned government attempts to make *Shari'ah* compliant finance more affordable by lower income Muslims may not have been what the higher end of the market wanted. This is only speculation, but comparison with the secular ethical sector does suggest that the recurrent assumption that lowering costs is all that is needed to make Islamic finance more popular may be mistaken.

There is thus a question mark over how such status-seeking consumer behaviour would be affected by the appearance of genuinely mass market Islamic or 'ethical' goods and services. Some answers to this question are likely to be provided by the expansion of the Co-operative Bank, discussed in Chapter 2, 'Retail Banking'. The expanded Co-operative will be the first bank branded as 'ethical' with a generally accessible branch network and full service provision. Early indications are that some customers of Lloyds who are being involuntarily transferred to the Co-operative are far from happy about becoming customers of what they perceive as a smaller and less reliable bank and do not find its ethical status in any way reassuring.[1] On the other hand, it can be imagined that many long-standing account holders of the Co-operative who made this choice in a conscious attempt to position themselves as more ethical consumers may not be happy to find that in future nobody will be able to tell whether they made this choice for themselves or were just transferred from Lloyds. There may be some implications here for the future of the Islamic Bank of Britain (IBB), which looks unlikely to be able to maintain a network of independent physical branches indefinitely and may eventually be absorbed by a larger bank. If that were to happen, care would need to be taken not to obscure the distinctive statement made by choosing an IBB account.

Neither Islamic nor any other form of ethical finance being offered at the present time makes a clear statement that helping the more deprived members of society is at the heart of what being ethical means. The main reason for this is of course that most providers are profit seeking and cannot afford to put poor people at the centre of their strategy. There is a real question about whether a focus on the disadvantaged can ever be compatible with making profits. It is evident that both observing ethical principles in a non-profit enterprise and making profit in a non-ethical enterprise are fairly straightforward. The more illuminating case studies are those which are able to combine profit-making with observing principles. A considerable number of the examples considered in this book do so, particularly in the area of investment fund management. It is debatable though how far an ethical model is compatible with having to pay heed to the interests of shareholders. Most of the case studies in this book which are profit-making re-invest their profits in the business, rather than having to pay shareholders. The advantage of a religiously prescribed system of ethics is that all shareholders are obliged to agree to it. When there is no such overriding authority the most ethically concerned shareholders are likely to find themselves under pressure from the less concerned. In this respect the secular ethical sector has more problems than the Islamic one.

Much of the ethical movement in finance and consumption is self-consciously counter-cultural. This is an important element in the self-image of those who embrace it and therefore of its marketing strategy, but by definition a reform movement cannot bring about fundamental and general change in an industry and remain counter-cultural. The only way to bring about an ethical transformation of the whole financial services industry, which is ostensibly what activists would like to see, is to appeal to the whole customer base, which means more or less the whole population. Small changes by large companies may have more impact on, say, the environment, or labour standards in developing countries, than grand gestures by small niche companies. It is also worth bearing in mind that large companies only have an incentive to improve their practices if they believe that a large proportion of their customers will continue to support them if they do but not if they do not. The element in the ethical finance movement which dislikes the whole conventional financial services industry so much that it wants nothing to do with it no matter how much it reforms cannot exert any pressure on providers, since they know that nothing they do will attract more custom from such people.

A particularly pertinent example here is that of the Church of England. However much the Christian tradition may idealise a non-materialistic philosophy of life, a penniless mystic would have no power at all to influence the practices of major companies. The Church on the other hand is able to exert a great deal of influence on the companies in which it invests and even on some in which it is merely considering investing, simply because the size of its holdings is so great. The entire holdings of all the investment funds branded as 'ethical' in the UK are said to be in the region of £11 billion. The Church of England on its own controls £8 billion of investments. The former prime minister Margaret Thatcher once commented that the Good Samaritan (a character in a Gospel parable who came to the aid of an injured man of a different ethnicity) was only able to do good because he had plenty of money as well as a kind disposition. She was much mocked for this remark at the time but there is a lot of truth in it. Islamic finance is sometimes regarded with suspicion by outsiders because of a perceived association with the wealth of the Arab oil states. There is so much potential for this wealth to be used to exert influence for good in societies in which Muslims are a minority, which is perhaps not being fully realised at present.

Conventional economics seeks to devise a system resilient to human weakness, while enthusiasts for Islamic economics often seem to be trying to make humans perfect. We hear a lot from them about *homo Islamicus* as the antithesis of *homo economicus,* the 'economic man' as conceived by classical economists. Religious writers reflexively reject the classical model of everyone being driven essentially by self-interest and motivated by the chance to make or save money, believing this to be much too cynical a view. However, there does not (after allowing for conspicuous consumption being a form of self-interest) seem to be very much evidence to disprove it. Even Islamic banks find that their clients are not prepared to tolerate low returns for the sake of religious compliance; this is the main reason why the banks are constantly pushing the limits of what scholars are prepared to approve. Secular ethical idealists come somewhere between these two extremes in their view of human nature. They do not usually entertain such lofty ideas of human perfectability as religious thinkers, but neither do they usually feel comfortable with economic theories based purely on self-interest and the pursuit of incentives. There is a need for a wide-ranging and serious discussion and exchange of ideas on these matters among all those who are dissatisfied with the limitations of the classical model.

Lessons for Islamic finance

The Islamic sector in the UK has distinctive problems if it wishes to become part of the wider movement seeking reform of banking. It has a vested interest in being able to portray conventional banking as unprincipled and thus to position itself as the principled alternative. If the conventional sector reformed itself to an extent where its most vociferous critics began to see it as an acceptable choice again, that would remove the ethical alternative's distinctive selling points. It may therefore be a risky strategy for Islamic finance to try too hard to position itself as just one ethical option among others. That might in the long run undermine its reason to exist. It will have a permanent reason to present itself as a principled alternative if it continues to emphasise that no other form of ethical finance shares all of its requirements.

This book has demonstrated the problems of definition and standardisation within the secular ethical sector. It would be a mistake for Islamic finance to try too hard to promote itself as part of a sector which is so poorly defined. It risks diluting the great strength of the Islamic sector in relation to secular alternatives, which is the rigour of its prescriptions and the formal and institutionalised structure of approval of all products by scholars. The negative side of this is that some ordinary Muslims are unhappy with being expected simply to accept the decision of the *Shari'ah* supervisory committee of their bank and not to exercise their own judgement on what is religiously acceptable. In the long run though Islamic finance may attract some 'concerned consumers' who have become dissatisfied with the more ephemeral nature of the ethical concerns of the wider world. Although Christianity does not have such clear prescriptions on economic matters as Islam, it does have a large body of theological thinking to draw on and refer to, which, again, may over time become a reference point in the confusion of the wider marketplace. There is probably more potential for fruitful exchanges between different religious traditions than between any of them and the secular examples, because what all religious traditions have in common is that they reject the belief that personal opinion can be the final arbiter of what is right.

It does however seem likely that Islamic banks will in future become more receptive to their customers' views both on interpretations of *Shari'ah* and on issues beyond the purely religious which the Muslim public would like to see them absorb. The Islamic sector could quite well accommodate such concerns as environmental issues and the pay and conditions of workers in overseas supply companies, without weakening its core strengths.

The Shukr Islamic Clothing company has not been discussed earlier in this book because it has no connection with financial services, and no judgement is implied here on whether it achieves its ideals in practice, but it has produced a well expressed statement of its 'vision' which indicates how Islamic companies can aspire to applying religious principles in every aspect of their work:

> Shukr also aspires to be a model Islamic business, by applying sacred Islamic values to a contemporary, multinational company. We follow fair trade and ethical labor [sic] practices, pursue a path of perfection by producing clothing of the

highest standards, and apply Islamic financial and investment principles, avoiding interest-based financing.[2]

This company's products are manufactured in Syria, which illustrates both the way that the traditional commercial strategy of reducing costs by moving production to low wage areas abroad can be targeted at Muslim majority countries and thus help to keep wealth within the *ummah*, and also the risks created by such an exposure to the more troubled parts of the Muslim world.

One of the most interesting aspects of the growth of Islamic financial services in the UK is the opportunities presented by it to develop innovative and high quality products which could be repatriated, as it were, to the Muslim majority world. Indeed this is a large part of the justification for this book: the interaction with other forms of ethical finance in the UK, where the ethical sector is probably more highly developed than anywhere else in the world, may eventually influence Islamic banking internationally. A limitation on this may be the significant differences between what is important to consumers in the UK and what is important in Muslim majority countries. Many of the concerns commonly found among 'concerned consumers' in the UK are what is sometimes referred to as 'post scarcity' consumer issues. For example, the citizens of countries which are still struggling with serious poverty and under-development cannot be expected to care that much about organic standards of food production; they are anxious to increase agricultural yields by any means.

Although issues of corporate governance have been prominent in public concerns about banking in Britain in recent years, the country has not experienced outright corruption on anything like the scale which is unfortunately common in some other countries, including some Muslim majority ones. The Ethical Corporation, a company which provides training for corporate clients on all of the matters usually embraced by the term 'ethical', reports that issues of corruption and corporate governance are a much greater concern for some of their overseas clients than they are accustomed to find with British clients.[3] This is a valuable reminder to keep a sense of perspective on the ethical issues with which British consumers are attempting to engage. On the whole it has not been necessary for them to campaign for an end to blatant fraud and dishonesty, because these matters are already well covered by the laws of the land. Legal tax avoidance by large companies does raise some legitimate ethical concerns, but it is not a moral issue in the same league as the private appropriation of public funds found in some Muslim majority countries. In this matter the ethical sector in the UK could learn something from the Islamic world about what to prioritise.

Islamic finance providers in the UK may find the trajectories of other religious minorities involved in banking instructive. The example of the banks founded by members of the Society of Friends (Quakers) was discussed in Chapter 2, 'Retail Banking'. The Society formed a small religious minority community with very close internal bonds, and this was conducive to success in business because of the dense networking and high level of trust among members. As Barclays and Lloyds succeeded and developed, they reached a size where the minority community of their founders was no longer the main influence on them and eventually became indistinguishable from other banks. The innovative energy is now coming from other minority religious groups, notably from Muslims but also from evangelical Christians, and from some environmentalist groups which could almost be classed as religious in their attitude to their 'green' ideology. (There is in fact an overlap between 'green' groups and what sociologists call 'new religious movements'.) The first generation of Muslim migrants to Britain had some of the same close community bonds as the early Quaker bankers, and were able to make substantial use of informal financial arrangements because of this. The Islamic banks which are now targeting the Muslim community in Britain have left those informal networks behind and grown to a size where they are just as impersonal and institutionalised as any other banks. It is to be hoped that they can be more successful than Barclays in retaining a distinctive character and ethos.

The future

The conventional political discourse about immigration in Britain has always centred on the expectation that incomers should adapt to their new country of residence in language and habits and demonstrate an undivided loyalty to it. This conventional expectation is being increasingly overtaken by the reality of the modern world, where being actively involved in more than one country is perfectly possible and being multilingual is a definite advantage. It is in particularly stark contrast with the nature of the financial services industry, which is the most transnational industry the world has ever seen. The financial services world is unapologetically global in its operations and concerns, and because banks deal in intangible products they can move their operations to another country very easily, guided only by the most advantageous tax and regulatory regimes.

When banking is globalised, so will the opposition to it be. The Occupy movement has made this very clear. Protest groups using this umbrella label appeared in many countries almost simultaneously, through the medium of the same online communications systems as have enabled the bankers themselves to operate internationally. While this particular movement lacked any sort of coherent ideology or concrete proposals for reform, the speed of its formation should be a warning of what might be possible in the future.

The only political groups which are consistent in expecting corporate as well as individual migrants to demonstrate patriotism are the more populist elements of the far right. We are reminded here that the term 'rootless cosmopolitans' used to have an anti-semitic sub-text, especially when applied to bankers. It is conceivable that Islamic banking may find itself targeted by a populist xenophobic political discourse if public anger at the behaviour of banks and at constant reductions in public spending continues to increase. It is also however entirely possible that the Islamic sector could play a valuable role during the period of hardship and transition which many in Britain are now facing, and that this could permanently change public perception of Islam and attract more people to the religion. In this context the example of Christians Against Poverty is pertinent. There is no reason why there could not be a Muslims Against Poverty group which could play a similar role among the poor. If those working in Islamic finance do not take this opportunity, it could take a long time to recover ground lost to other religions and to secular humanitarians.

Greater convergence and co-operation in the area of financial services in Britain would help to promote good inter-faith relations and increase interaction among different communities which are now largely segregated not only by religion but by very different levels of socio-economic attainment and opportunity. At the moment it seems to be Islamic charities which are the furthest advanced among Islamic enterprises in working with the wider society as well as the Muslim community and in transmitting the message about the fundamental principles of Islam to non-Muslims.

The centrality of the principle of mutualism to the Islamic tradition needs to be explained better to non-Muslims so that instead of just talking vaguely about 'values', both Islamic and non-Islamic workers for more equitable financial services can base their efforts on clearly conceptualised principles of co-operation, mutual support and sharing of risk. There are exciting possibilities for new financial models of great social benefit to emerge from such a pooling of ideas and experience.

Notes

1. Correspondents to *Moneybox*, broadcast on BBC Radio 4 on 15 December 2012. Those who doubted the viability of the Co-operative Bank's purchase of the Lloyds branches must have felt vindicated when, in April 2013, while this book was in press, the Co-operative announced its decision not to proceed with the arrangement.
2. www.shukr.co.uk (accessed on 18 December 2012).
3. 'The Smarter Business Blog' on 15 November 2012, at www.tobywebb.blogspot.co.uk.

GLOSSARY AND ABBREVIATIONS

da'wah	literally the 'call' or 'invitation' to Islam, Islamic proselytism
gharar	sometimes translated as 'speculation' but also covers a wide range of contractual uncertainties; one of the main prohibitions in Islamic economic thought
halaal	'permitted', in accordance with Islamic teaching
haraam	'forbidden', unacceptable in Islam
ijarah	a form of leasing contract, the most popular model of Islamic home purchase finance
mudarabah	a form of business finance where one party supplies the capital and the other the labour or entrepreneurial initiative and profits are shared in agreed proportions
murabahah	a combination of contracts for purchase and immediate re-sale at a higher price, a common form of Islamic financing
musharakah	a form of business finance where two or more parties contribute capital to a venture and share the profits in agreed proportions
rab al-maal	literally 'the master of the money', the person who supplies the capital in a *mudarabah* contract
riba	an unacceptable form of increase of capital, usually identified with bank interest; the

	most important prohibition in Islamic economic thought
sadaqah	any form of voluntary charitable giving, distinct from *zakat*
Shari'ah	literally the 'path' of Islam, the entire body of principles which constitutes the religion of Islam; often translated as 'Islamic law' but it is not comparable to a secular legal code
sukuk	a form of financial instrument which serves a similar function to bonds and bills in conventional finance; the word is the plural form of *sakk* but is often used in English as if it were a singular noun
takaful	'mutual assurance', a form of Islamic insurance
tawhid	the unity and indivisibility of God; the most fundamental concept in Islam
tzedakah	the payment of 10 per cent of one's income to good causes required in Judaism; tithing is the Christian version of this
ummah	the entire Muslim community worldwide
waqf	a gift of property in perpetuity to a charitable cause
zakat	the 2.5 per cent of one's wealth above a certain threshold (*nisab*) which must be donated to charity annually

ABCUL	Association of British Credit Unions Limited
CAP	Christians Against Poverty
EIRIS	Ethical Investment Research Services
ESG	environmental, social and governance
FSA	Financial Services Authority
HMRC	Her Majesty's Revenue and Customs, the United Kingdom taxation authority
IBB	Islamic Bank of Britain
ISA	Individual Savings Account, a tax-free way of saving in the UK
Libor	London Inter Bank Offer Rate of interest
NCUL	Northumberland Credit Union Limited
NS&I	National Savings and Investments
OFT	Office of Fair Trading
RBS	Royal Bank of Scotland
UKSIF	United Kingdom Sustainable Investment and Finance Association

INDEX